PLANET

OF

THE

BLIND

Stephen Kuusisto

Delta
Trade Paperbacks

A Delta Book
Published by
Dell Publishing
a division of
Bantam Doubleday Dell Publishing Group, Inc.
1540 Broadway
New York, New York 10036

Copyright © 1998 by Stephen Kuusisto

ISBN 0-385-33327-7

Reprinted by arrangement with The Dial Press

Manufactured in the United States of America
Published simultaneously in Canada

January 1999

10 9 8 7 6 5 4 3 2 1

BVG

HIGH PRAISE FOR STEPHEN KUUSISTO'S
PLANET OF THE BLIND

"Historically, the blind have been endowed with divine judgment and magical power. Kuusisto is a bearer of such insight and enchantment. In his breathtaking memoir, he creates a world of brilliance, color and fertile imaginings. . . . In *Planet of the Blind*, the ordinary is miraculous."

—*San Francisco Chronicle*

"EXQUISITELY OBSERVED . . . BEAUTIFULLY POETIC . . . a gripping and literary narrative, loaded with unusual metaphoric language, the kind that startles in its descriptive power and brings the reader persuasively to an unfamiliar place."

—*The New York Times Book Review*

"THE SHEER BEAUTY OF KUUSISTO'S WRITING creates a miraculous planet: a swirl of sensation and nuanced perception, ecstasy, terror, and love. Here a soul on a bicycle is propelled by pure desire. And here we, in turn, are propelled toward a new vision."

—Andrea Barrett, author of *Ship Fever*

"A LUMINOUS MEMOIR OF A DARKENED WORLD . . . a remarkable journey, funny at times, infuriating at others, yet rarely encumbered by self-pity."

—*The Boston Globe*

"EVERY PAGE OF THIS EXTRAORDINARY BOOK IS WORTH REFINGERING AND REREADING. It's as if the whole thing has been rubbed in gold dust: the prose has a richness not often found in poetry, let alone in memoirs by first-time writers, let alone in memoirs by first-time writers who happen to be blind."

—*The Guardian*

"KUUSISTO'S WRITING IS A JOY: clear, poetic and embellished with wonderful imagery. His poetry has given him extra sight. He writes of 'colours and shapes that are windblown'; waiting in the grocery store, he lives inside a Jackson Pollock painting. He sees things, not only Grand Central Station, as 'beautiful and useless.' I almost feel: lucky man."

—*The Sunday Times* (London)

Please turn the page for more extraordinary acclaim. . . .

*For Connie, Carol, and Michelle, my Guiding Hearts,
and for Corky, my Guiding Eyes*

In an effort to safeguard the privacy of
several individuals, the author has
changed their names and, in some cases,
disguised identifying characteristics or
created composite characters.

PLANET
OF
THE
BLIND

Prologue

I'VE ENTERED Grand Central Station with guide dog Corky, my yellow Labrador. We stand uncertain, man and dog collecting our wits while thousands of five o'clock commuters jostle around us. Beside them, Corky and I are in slow motion, like two sea lions. We've suddenly found ourselves in the ocean, and here in this railway terminal, where pickpockets and knife artists roam the crowds, we're moving in a different tempo. There is something about us, the perfect poise of the dog, the uprightness of the man, I don't know, a spirit maybe, fresh as the gibbous moon, the moon we've waited for, the one with the new light.

So this is our railway station, a temple for Hermes. We wash through the immense vault with no idea about how to find our train or the information kiosk. And just now it doesn't matter. None of the turmoil or anxiety of being lost will reach us because moving is holy, the very motion is a breeze from Jerusalem.

This blindness of mine still allows me to see colors and shapes that seem windblown; the great terminal is supremely lovely in its swaying hemlock darknesses and sudden pools of rose-colored electric light. We don't know where we are, and though the world is dangerous, it's also haunting in its beauty. Even to a lost man with a speck of something like seeing, this minute here, just standing, taking in the air as a living circus, this is what tears of joy are for.

A railway employee has offered to guide me to my train. I hold his elbow gently, Corky heeling beside us, and we descend through the tunnels under the building. I've decided to trust a stranger.

Welcome to the planet of the blind.

I

—

THE
VILLAGE
of St. Ovide

"For Sun and Moon supply their conforming masks, but in this hour of civil twilight all must wear their own faces."

—W. H. Auden,
"Horae Canonicae"

1

—

BLINDNESS IS OFTEN perceived by the sighted as an either/or condition: one sees or does not see. But often a blind person experiences a series of veils: I stare at the world through smeared and broken windowpanes. Ahead of me the shapes and colors suggest the sails of Tristan's ship or an elephant's ear floating in air, though in reality it is a middle-aged man in a London Fog raincoat that billows behind him in the April wind. He is like the great dead Greeks in Homer's descriptions of the underworld. In the heliographic distortions of sunlight or dusk, everyone I meet is crossing Charon's river. People shimmer like beehives.

I was born in the Exeter, New Hampshire, hospital three months prematurely, in March 1955. My identical twin brother lived exactly one day. Taken together we weighed five pounds, but with the death of my twin, my own weight dropped. My chances of survival were thought to be minimal; I was incubated and given oxygen. Within a week my weight stabilized, and then I began to grow.

Many children born prematurely in the fifties and early sixties suffer from visual impairments. The condition (which still exists, though it is less common today) is known as the "retinopathy of prematurity." The tiny blood vessels of the retinas are formed in the last trimester of pregnancy, so if a child is born prematurely, the retinas are often underdeveloped. In the fifties incubators were overly oxygenated, which further complicated the retinopathy—babies incubated with too much oxygen would routinely go blind. In my case the retinas were scarred.

Nystagmus is an additional complication of "ROP." My eyes dart uncontrollably and often appear to be jumping in my head. Such "darting eyes" make it nearly impossible to focus. I was also born with strabismus, or crossed eyes, and though later surgery would try to correct this, the operation was only an aesthetic exercise—I never gained muscle control over my eyes.

20/200 is the definition of legal blindness. What a normal person sees from a distance of two hundred feet, the blind person will see from twenty. In childhood my best visual correction was 20/200 in my left eye. With that eye I had enough muscle control to place my nose on a piece of paper and perhaps make out something if the print was dark and large. Up until the age of forty I could do this for a half hour at a time. Later, inoperable cataracts made this impossible. From the beginning my right eye couldn't read and would hop like a starling in a hedge, recording glimpses of color at the tip of my nose.

The sensorium of the blind who possess some marginal vision is by turns magical and disturbing. There is nothing in front of you, nothing behind. Now there is a shadow in the shape of a man who has appeared from the mist. How lovely and terrible this is! It's a mad, holy vision, the repeated appearance and disappearance of the physical world.

My sister once spent some time in meditation at a Hindu ashram in the south of Germany and came home having seen the very air atomize into a dazzling whirlwind of living particles. Hearing her story, I thought of walking alone at dawn, the morning light like stained glass. I can see these things as I walk to the corner store for milk. It's like living inside an immense abstract painting. Jackson Pollock's drip canvas *Blue Poles* comes to mind, a tidal wash, an enormous, animate cloud filled with light. This is glacial seeing, like lying on your back in an ice cave and staring up at the cobalt sun.

The beauty is of course conditional. Many who have minimal sight are photophobic, like myself, and daylight is painful. I can't go outdoors without wearing the darkest possible glasses. When I enter a shop or restaurant, I am totally blind. When my eyes have adjusted, I still cannot read a menu or catch the eye of a waiter. My eyes dance in a private, rising field of silver threads, teeming greens, roses, and smoke.

Such waltzing is not easy. Raised to know I was blind but taught to disavow it, I grew bent over like the dry tinder grass. I couldn't stand up proudly, nor could I retreat. I reflected my mother's complex bravery and denial and marched everywhere at dizzying speeds without a cane. Still, I remained ashamed of my blind self, that blackened dolmen. The very words *blind* and *blindness* were scarcely to be spoken around me. I would see to this by my exemplary performance. My mother would avoid the word, relegating it to the province of cancer.

Given my first pair of glasses at the age of three, I carried them in secret to the garden and buried them under the wide leaves of a rhubarb plant. A year later the glasses were discovered by the family that was subletting our house while my parents and I traveled to Scandinavia. They couldn't imagine how these tiny gold-framed spectacles had been interred in the earth.

Once when I was nine or ten, my sister Carol, who is four years younger than I am, came home from school in a state of inspiration. She had read a book in class about a young woman who went blind and then found her life renewed with the help of a guide dog. Carol recalls how I threw snow at her as she pretended to be blind with the help of our family's golden retriever. I ran behind her, stinging her with ice.

Who would choose to be blind?

■　■　■

I WOULD CONQUER space by hurtling through it. I wore telescopic glasses, suffered from crushing headaches, but still chose to ride a bicycle—with nothing more than adrenaline for assurance.

How do you ride a bicycle when you can't see? You hold your head like a stiff flower and tilt toward the light. You think not at all about your chances—the sheer physicality of gutters and pavements. One submits to Holy Rule and spins ahead.

Picture this: A darkness rises. Is it a tree or a shadow? A shadow or a truck? The thrill of the high wire is the greatest wonder of the brain. There is, at the center of our skulls, a terrible glittering, a requiem light. I lower my face to the cold handlebars and decide it's a shadow, a hole in sunlight, and pedal straight through.

Here's another shadow, and another. I turn sharply but this time plunge into tall weeds. Insects rise into my hair, cling to my sweaty face. From the road comes the hiss of angered gravel, a car roars past. Thanks be to God! I'm alive in the wild carrot leaf!

I let a bee walk along my wrist, feel it browse on my perspiration. The bicycle coasts, and I squint in the glare, and then I hit a root. As I fall, I take the sting of bee, then the sting of cement. My glasses fly off. The only thing I wonder is whether I've been seen. Nothing with this boy must be amiss! He *belongs* on the street!

Now I'm on my knees groping for the glasses. My wrist has swollen. One wheel is still spinning. I've barely struck the ground, and my fingers are everywhere. I must find the glasses before anyone sees me. No one must know how evanescent is my seeing. No one must know how dangerous my cycling really is.

And then there are shadows surrounding me. Please let these blurs not be children!

Yes! The shadows are trees.

Now I touch the glasses, heft them back to my face. They are heavy as padlocks.

Quickly I raise the bicycle and straighten it.

I ride.

In a mathematical world there are so many factors: Were my years of cycling an actuarial gift? Who else was on the road as I was cycling in the opposite direction? Did I stop on the true day of terminus, the day when my numbers were up?

I cycled from the age of ten until I was thirty. During my last decade it was occasional, more furtive, a headless activity like taking drugs. By my twenties, I knew it was injurious. As a child, I had only that graven need to resemble.

Of course my mother gave me this bicycle in the first place, a gift made from her guilt. I love her for the gift of speed and remain angry because of it. Mine was a boyhood of thrills and nausea.

• • •

MY FAMILY SETS sail for Scandinavia aboard the SS *Stockholm* in 1958. We travel to Helsinki so my father, a professor of government at the University of New Hampshire, can study the cold war through the medium of Finnish politics. I am three years old, and I've already buried my first pair of glasses.

Aboard the *Stockholm* I elude my mother by running wildly. At that age I am already the dervish of labyrinths. No adult can confine me to a stateroom. On "D" deck I become the mascot of a sailors' card game. The red tiles of the lower decks and the white tunics of the sailors swirl like the walls of a funhouse. How do I avoid falling down a gangway? I recall the dazzling machinery of the engine room as a storm of color.

In Helsinki I lean close to the gray, birdlike women with ether eyes who ride the trams. Each has survived the wartime starvation, and now, in the darkest city on earth, they are riding home with their satchels, which had taken all day to fill; the stores were ill-stocked and the lines were long. I remember their almost feral attention to the trolley's windows at twilight. As a small boy, I climb ever closer to them, their strangeness imprinting on me an indelible image of hardship.

One day, climbing the stairs with my father in our apartment building, we meet a severe old woman who speaks to my father in Finland's brand of Swedish. I am acutely aware that I am the object of scrutiny. She points with a cane:

"Tsk tsk," she says, "*barna*-blind—blind child."

Her voice echoes on the stairs, "*barna*-blind"—blind from birth. I was not quite sighted; I wished to never be blind. Didn't this old crone know that I'd buried my first pair of glasses under the rhubarb? This will be a nearly lifelong puzzle for me: Am I not a sighted boy? Am I not attempting bravely to see? What must I do?

I know that I don't belong anywhere, so I become the spindrift of ocean liners, streetcars, and stairwells. I must have driven my mother insane. That year I survived on banana ice cream cones, which I extorted my parents to buy from the streetcorner dairy stands. I could see their effulgent red and blue awnings and quickly learned to make vocal my need for ice cream in loud Finnish so as to inspire my parents with the stares of the crowds.

Delicate, skinny, inordinately active, I was sharpening a sixth sense that fostered the impression in my parents and almost everyone else that I could see far better than I really could. Such acting requires a capacious memory; in the gauzy nets of pastel colors where I lived, every inch of terrain had to be acutely remembered. In the heart of every blooming and buzzing confusion, I found a signpost, something to guide me back along my untutored path. Twenty-one years later, when I returned to Helsinki with my own Fulbright grant, I found the door of our old apartment building by following the dropped bread crumbs of the blind child's choreography.

Even today I live in the "customs house" between the land of the blind and those who possess some minor capacity to see. It's a transitory place, its foundation shifting, its promise of stasis always suspect. There are moments when I see better than others since conditions of light are peremptory and loaded with impact. The whims of architects have enormous power over my experience of vision: a postmodern shopping mall with its cantilevered floors and mirrored walls—all lit by indirect lighting and high-intensity bulbs—can reduce my momentum. The darkness of restaurants and bars tightens my chest. I edge along without poise, feeling the sudden reverberations of alarm that come with not seeing. In a room designed for urbane and sexy people, I feel the boyhood panic, imagining myself an old man holding objects close to his face. How does one become inured to unpredictable moments of helplessness? I turn a corner into direct sunlight, and without warning I'm the boy grasping at tremendous air.

I remember Helsinki's open-air fish market, where I ran through the crowds of winter shoppers. The green and gold of vegetables and fruits, and the icy chill of the butchers' stalls where the walls were bloodred—all of it drew me on and on. I could run in abandon bouncing off strangers, wild to elude my mother and absorb the colors. The market became my customs house between the ocean of blindness and the land of seeing.

■ ■ ■

BACK IN THE States, my mother must fight with the local district to gain my admission to an ordinary first-grade classroom. I am a legally blind child, and it is the era of Kennedy. It will be another thirty years before people with disabilities are guaranteed their civil rights in the United States.

I am emphatically told not to mix. In some cases this comes from the parents, who think I might break during ordinary play.

"The kids are playing rough now, so why don't you come over here with us?"

I sit in a lawn chair while my mother's friends take in the sun and the fragrance of suntan lotion mixes with their cigarettes.

Mrs. O'Daly lets me sip her coffee, although there is some joking about stunting growth.

"You don't want to play with them, they're nasty," one mother opines, with a stream of smoke.

"You're better off right here!"

There is laughter at this. It's true: I'm better off hiding behind the lawn chair. But I can hear their children through the trees, the shrieks and exaggerations.

"Why don't you tell them to play with me?" For this, there is no answer, only the hasty decision to change a baby or "start on supper."

In our town there are no discernible men or women with disabilities, with the exception of World War II veterans. A disabled child is without a category: one simply doesn't see them. My mother, in turn, believes that I should live like other children—at least as much as possible. It's a decision that must make her as lonely as her son. There are no books about blind children or how to bring them up, no associations of parents or support materials, at least not in rural New Hampshire. Instead there are assumptions: Blindness is a profound misfortune, a calamity really, for ordinary life can't accommodate it. For my parents this puzzle will be even harder because my vision loss is a form of "legal blindness"—a confusing phrase that means that I can see fractionally, though not enough to truly see. Not enough to drive or operate machinery or read an ordinary book.

So I am blind in a bittersweet way: I see like a person who looks through a kaleidoscope; my impressions of the world are at once beautiful and largely useless.

The one thing my parents know for certain is that blindness is stigmatized. Fearing for my financial security, my father tries to buy a life insurance policy in my name, only to find that blindness is an impediment. That same year my mother decides to enroll me in public school instead of an institution for the blind and finds both consternation and disapproval from school and staff officials.

So on a hot August day we are visited by a social worker. We live at the end of a forested dead-end road in Durham, a road of screaming blue jays and orange daylilies. A black sedan stops in front of our house, and a heavy woman climbs out with the help of the driver. Then she unfolds her white cane and makes her way to our door. My mother is roused both by a horror of blindness and incipient hostility for bureaucracy. Who are they to say her son is blind? He mustn't be seen in the company of a blind social worker—the stigma might be impossible to erase.

I'm sent to the cellar. There I find a piano, a toy chest, a variety of amusements. The cellar doesn't feel like a banishment, but I know something's up. I stay at the top of the stairs, my ear to the door.

The muffled sound of adults in dispute is a terrible thing for a child. Beyond the cellar door I hear their gloomy voices as they argue about where I should be in the world. That argument has never ended for me: on that day over thirty-six years ago, both were approximately correct. The social worker says I am too blind for the public schools of the day. My mother counters that I wouldn't have the same kind of social experience at a blind institute. "Those places teach kids how to cane chairs," she says. The blind woman insists that I won't learn braille in a public school, won't learn to use a white cane. My mother cannot accept that these are real drawbacks—she takes this as further proof that I should be enrolled in the public school system. Hers is an urgent and primitive choice, one that today would be unnecessary as blind children regularly attend public schools and receive cane, travel, and braille lessons at the same time.

Blind though I am, my mother is hell-bent on emphasizing my small window of vision. I am going to be dimly sighted and "normal." According to her, I will damn well ride a bike and go sledding, and do whatever the hell else ordinary children do. To her the prospect of the white cane denotes the world of the invalid.

But I need that cane. I am about to begin an impossible contest with the sighted world, a display that today is known as "passing" or more correctly, "trying to pass."

It's hard to explain how, as a child, or even as a grown man, I have been so proficient at hurtling forward without breaking my neck. To those watching, it must seem as if I see. My blind friend Peter, who has never seen anything but darkness, moves the same way. I suppose this plummeting through the world involves the same inexplicable faith known to skydivers. Fast blind people have exceptional memories and superior spatial orientation. By the age of five, I was a dynamo. Wanting to see me run, my mother saw me run and guessed that I must be seeing more than I really could. And so I landed like the bee who sees poorly but understands destination by motion and light and temperature.

I turn and climb down the stairs, remembering to avoid the canning jars and Sears catalogs. I'm headed for the ancient mahogany upright piano. It's music I'm after; I'm already entranced by the keys. In my grandmother's attic I'd turned the handle of a Victrola and discovered Caruso, a voice like milk and iodine pouring from inside a paper horn. In our own house I listen to my father's Tchaikovsky records, running my fingertips over the cloth facing of the electric speaker.

When the social worker leaves, my mother does not come to find me. Instead she goes to her own room and sleeps with the curtains drawn.

I stay at the piano for hours.

After supper I go outside and shout in the empty road in the hope that some kids will play with me.

Later, alone in the woods, wet elbowed and wet kneed, I catch my trousers on a sunken rock, lean into the ground, press my chin into the moss. The things I see are an alembic of distilled colors and shapes.

"Heaven," says Robert Frost "gives its glimpses only to those / Not in position to look too close."

I push my face into the fireweed.

2

—

BY THE AGE of five, I've been in and out of hospitals. The muscles around my eyes have been cut and stitched as a means of correcting my strabismus. After the surgery I have bandages on my eyes for several months, and that is when I learn to hear. I spend whole afternoons listening. I can hear the wooden gears of the railroad clock that hangs on the far wall.

The strabismus operation has made me appear less cross-eyed, though the eyes move independently, and in their separate depths of color they afford me nothing like depth perception or balance. By now my glasses are extremely thick. They allow me to make use of my delicate residual vision, but they're cumbersome and painful to wear, and the target of teasing by other children.

On the first day of school the teacher, Mrs. Edinger, posts a photograph above the blackboard; two chubby infants swaddled in diapers stare down on the class. Those who are caught whispering will have their names appended under the babies' curled feet.

"This is the Baby Board," says Mrs. Edinger, "and anyone who talks out of turn will have their name put here. Only babies talk when they're supposed to be quiet!"

When I enter the public school, I am without assistance. Without "low vision" specialists or special education standards, I am without the benefits of proper orientation and mobility training. There are no braille lessons for me, no large print materials. The air flashes like quartz, and I see nothing of the arithmetic lesson. My fingers slide in all directions. I clasp and unclasp the lid of my pencil box, trace the scars on my desk. I pull at my eyelids in an effort to refine the mist.

I must ask a question, some nearly useless thing like how many dogs are on the blackboard. I turn to Janet, who sits next to me, and whisper, "How many dogs are there?"

"I see Stephen talking!" cries the teacher, and there is the staccato of chalk in action. "Stephen's name goes on the Baby Board!"

I am swollen shut, catch myself, sit straight in my chair as laughter breaks around me.

Without an assistant I am forced to listen.

I listen like a person telephoning in the dark.

I listen like the ornithologist who unwraps bird bones from tissue paper.

■ ■ ■

EACH MORNING MRS. Edinger begins the day with a Bible story. Here come jawbones, slings, infants floating in baskets, a lion's den, and a trapped man. Now she recites frankincense and myrrh, robes of gold, a nativity star.

Everything comes to me by repetition.

On the playground I lean against a wall, immured by the strings of words that have accumulated during the morning. Around me my classmates are playing a game loosely called Kill the Germans—they race through the November mire letting out shrieks. There is a great deal of arguing about who is dead. Sometimes I lower my head like a fullback and run right through them.

Back in the classroom, I count imaginary frogs, butterflies, spacemen, following the lessons without usable print or concrete numbers. The world is skewed according to the compensatory pictures flashing through my head. I follow the teacher's words and make a kind of caged progress, trapped as I am in my own neural nets.

One day Mrs. Edinger posts a photograph of astronauts above the blackboard.

"Astronauts orbit the earth," she says, "and you can only be an astronaut if you are very good at your lessons."

Students who finish their in-class assignments before the rest will henceforth be "astronauts"—permitted to orbit the classroom and peer over the shoulders of the others.

John Glenn has just orbited the planet, sailing upright from sunrise to sunset within an hour. A television has been wheeled into our classroom, and I listen to Walter Cronkite, who is sufficiently loud even for the dead.

Now as I press my nose to an impossible page, trying to read some inscription in the dust of damaged retinas, here comes a kid to loom over me. He is orbiting.

"Hey," he murmurs, "get a little closer!" and he shoves my nose into the paper before passing down the row of desks.

Later, playing alone, I pretend to be Walter Cronkite, shuffling unreadable pages. The attic is my television studio.

I sit under the sloping eaves, and with rain on the roof for accompaniment, I talk to my audience.

■ ■ ■

IN SCHOOL THE printed word scurries away from my one "reading eye"—words in fact seem to me like insects released from a box. While the class reads aloud, I watch the spirals of hypnotic light that ripple across my eyes when I move them from side to side. I do not belong here. My little body at this desk is something uncanny—a thing that belongs in the darkness and that has been brought to daylight.

But I talk, answer questions, make others laugh. I'm interested in everything and tell the class that I can spell Tchaikovsky.

Mrs. Edinger, she of the Astronaut Board, becomes the first saint in my life. She takes it upon herself to help me read. After school we sit at her desk, and with my nose jammed into the pages, we go over the words. And though I'm squinting and struggling supremely over each alphabetic squiggle, she has the patience of an archaeologist, one who dusts the microscopic shards before putting them away. With her, I hold my eye very still and make out the words.

Years later I learn from my mother that Mrs. Edinger is a black woman and perhaps the first person of African American heritage to teach in this local New Hampshire school. We are mutual explorers as we go over the hopeless print. She's noticed my determination and has figured out that I have a photographic memory. This probably contributes to her desire to see me read—she knows I'll retain the words that I've struggled so hard to grasp.

Hours of after-school time are spent before I can match the class in reading. I have to hold my book an inch from my eye and try hard to hold the hot, spasming muscle. The exhaustion of this is like the deep fatigue drivers feel after being too long on the road. The ordinary effort of reading is, for me, a whole-body experience. My neck, shoulders, and, finally, my lower back contract with pain. The legally blind know what it is to be old: even before the third grade I am hunched and shaking with effort, always on the verge of tears, seeing by approximation, craving a solid sentence. Then the words dissolve or run like ants. Nevertheless I find a lighted room inside my head, a place for self-affiliation. I am not blind, am not the target of pranks.

But leaving my reading lesson, a boy I think of as a friend steals my glasses and my panic brings me alive like a tree filled with birds: I navigate with my hands.

"Hey, Blindo, over here!"

He laughs along with several others, then they run.

I lunge with my arms straight following the sounds of sneakers. I'm determined not to cry: steel keys revolve and lock in my brain. Then I trip on a curb and cut my hands on a storm drain.

To this day I picture that boy clutching my glasses at a safe distance and watching me drift about. I learned early that with my glasses I'm blind, without them I'm a wild white face, a body groping, the miner who's come suddenly into the light.

On this particular afternoon I am instantly put on display. Now, in one stroke, I am a jellyfish, measureless and unwieldy. More than thirty years have passed since that moment, but I'm still disconcerted by what it felt like to belong so thoroughly to other people, to be, in effect, their possession. There should be a book of etiquette for those who find themselves in the predicament of the monster. Robbed of my glasses, I was no longer an impaired boy who'd been barred from sports. Instead I was amphibious.

I suppose he must have thrown the glasses to the ground and run away. Probably an adult was coming; I can't remember now.

■ ■ ■

BY THE THIRD grade, I'm wearing glasses fitted with telescopes and am promptly labeled "Martian." My anxieties live like pilot birds atop my shoulders. I pull all the hair from my eyebrows. Other kids call me Magoo over and over again.

In the sixties, Mr. Magoo is the latest descendant in a long line of comic blind characters playing the role of the sighted man. Valentin Hauy, an eighteenth-century French educator and the first great benefactor of the blind, witnessed one such spectacle in 1771. A group of blind men were arranged in the village square of St. Ovide, all of them dressed like clowns, each wearing a dunce's cap. These are the people who unwittingly expose themselves, who can't control their hands.

Hauy saw them in the village square, each carrying a musical instrument—a fiddle, a horn, a hand organ. On their faces the town magistrate had placed large cardboard cut-out spectacles. Placed before them on a desk were lanterns and sheets of music that the men made burlesque attempts at reading by playing their instruments, with predictable results. The villagers found this amusing enough to keep the show going for several weeks. When the musicians could no longer make money, they returned to their lives of begging. But their concert gives Magoo a comic pedigree.

In a magazine advertisement for the Blue Cross/Blue Shield

health insurance companies, "Mr. Magoo" is a bald little blind man whose tightly shut eyes look like question marks. There's no attempt in any representation of Magoo to cover his eyes with dark glasses.

In the advertisement Mr. Magoo is driving down a hill in an antiquated car. He's blissfully unaware that he's crossing the railway tracks. He mutters about the "potholes" as he drives across, just ahead of an oncoming train. Magoo is like Charlie Chaplin, who, blindfolded, circles the edge of a precipice on roller skates. His power resides in his luck, which is angelic. His every arrival is a miracle.

When Mr. Magoo drives a car, America's television audience experiences the same comic frisson as Hauy's villagers who laughed at the beggars wearing cardboard spectacles. But the blind are seldom depicted as being more than this. They are blind fools, or conversely, they're suddenly cosmic.

• • •

ASHAMED OF MY telescopes, I hide them in drawers and walk about with my head tipped slightly to the left to gain more refraction from my heavy prismatic glasses. I take to spending hours in attics or barns, places filled with tools and broken machinery.

My world is full of particulars, a glass case in a provincial museum. Here's a black dancing slipper with glued crimson feathers; a ballpoint pen from the Marcellus Casket Company. I'm nailed down with curios. But even the nearest things are evasive; objects buzz as in early motion pictures. Even as I wish to see, to pass for one who sees, that sight is eluding me.

In a neighbor's shed I stand at the dusty keys of an upright piano and count how many have lost their ivory—two black keys are missing. And mice or moths have long since feasted on the purple felt that lines the back of the keyboard. I hear wasps striking windows, and a hand mower, and somewhere far off a radio tuned to a baseball game. But I am absorbed in the colors and odors of this instrument, which looms over me like a wreck, the hull that Robinson Crusoe returned to. I am drawn by its worn pedals, the pegs and hammers, the cast iron frame, and the sour metallic scent of its dead strings.

I press my nose to everything. I look perpetually like a mendicant on Ash Wednesday.

I draw the skeleton of a catfish across the bridge of my glasses.

I go to the woods and sit on the mossy ledge of a great stone. As blue turns to black, the sky is momentarily transparent. I am skating there, turning my head sharply, intuiting the next place to rest my forehead.

■ ■ ■

MY SISTER IS a true friend, a collector of shining oddities, a woman's shoe containing a daddy longlegs and a moth that she has found in a dusty corner of the garage.

We spend the afternoon building a votive temple around this insect sarcophagus. For guards we have a stuffed lion, a flesh-colored plastic figurine of Tarzan, a Raggedy Ann doll wearing a red skirt. I need someone to bring me objects and say "Look at this!" My sister doesn't seem to notice that I have to place each thing up against my jumping eyes. She's oblivious to her brother's resemblance to Franz Kafka as a kid—a child whose eyes can't look straight.

Some years ago I came across a photograph of Kafka at the age of five. The photo shows that he had a wandering eye, or what doctors call a "lazy eye." Though he's trying to look at the camera, he seems lost. He's dressed like a circus ringmaster. Behind him is an animal with the head of a sheep, though its hindquarters and tail suggest something of the dog. It has a bridle and saddle, as though it's meant to be ridden. This is a photographer's studio creature, something from the workshop of an odd cobbler. Kafka looks at home with the creature; his world is routinely a place of ill-defined animals, of things that are not what they seem.

I imagine he sees blue smoke. Faces loom, adults are rising from the vista like sensate stones. These are the gorgeous mirages of not-seeing, moments red and green and black as the studios of Matisse. The moments are seriocomic: a white horse stands at the circus, no, it's a bedsheet in the wind.

I, too, went to the circus. Under the great Barnum tent, the lion tamer—Clyde Beatty in a two-story iron cage—appears like the Duke of Mantua, fighting three leopards with a chair and whip. All this I did not see. What I did see was the pink floodlit haze where that cage stood, heard the crack of a whip, the roar of the cats. The faces of the children and adults who surrounded me in the raised wooden bleachers were lit as though their cotton candy contained glowworms. But beyond this, wherever I looked, the concentration of the colors flew apart, the kaleidoscope circus fog of Gypsy tints and shadows flooded me.

I watched the face of my uncle, a heavy, simian, unshaven man, one who was not given to smiling. He studied the drama of Clyde Beatty, his expression as intense as that of the immigrant who has sighted shore at last. Around his head floated smoke rings from his expensive cigar. He told me at last that the cats were lying down. The crowd was wild. When I looked toward the cage, I saw astral lava, a pink hurricane of cigar-lit stage lights, and then the gold flash of what I took to be the whip.

Unable to see, I watched appearances abound, and while the animals were too far away, the harlequin masks of family loomed around me. Like the boyish Kafka, I smiled.

3

THROUGHOUT CHILDHOOD MY glasses grow thicker and thicker. My twice-a-year visits to the ophthalmologist are trips to the underworld. We enter from the midsummer brilliance into a thickly curtained room, its walls lined with high mahogany cabinets, each containing a thousand lenses. Then there is the examining chair, which rises like a dark sphinx but with many arms. After some small talk between the doctor and my parents, the chair does rise, carrying my head into a forest of mechanisms, a place of altitude, piercing lights, and tiny probes.

The doctor's hands smell of antiseptic and cigarettes. There is a hint of starch from his cotton lab coat. His face looms against mine, and sometimes our foreheads touch as he peers intently into my left eye. A mosaic of microscopic blue stones soars inside my skull, a blue that I've never found in the outer world.

Quickly the blue gives way to red: a spiraling web of blood and winter branches, the reflection of the inner eye before the re-lentless examination light.

On the eye chart I make out the big E, and from then on it's guesswork. The doctor procures lens after lens from the cabinets as if they were mounted butterflies and holds them to my face. I see roseate rings of color, rainbow reflections from the thick glass, but try though I may, I can't climb down those oscillating tunnels of promised clarity.

Throughout the exam I am talked about in the third person: "He doesn't seem to distinguish between lens one and two, let's not change his prescription for now."

And I am led back into the light of day, a light that scours my entire being. The dilating drops last all day, and so I must stay inside in a curtained room. Around in a ring I fly, diving through the hour with the radio. Listening to baseball, I drift above the green shell of Fenway Park, the blind boy in his dirigible, newly arrived from provinces unheard of since the age of the pharaohs: I eat apples in the dark and spend the entire day alone.

■ ■ ■

MY MOTHER DECIDES that I should take typing lessons, and so while the other fourth-grade students are saying the Pledge of Allegiance, I go each morning to a curtained alcove in the school nurse's office, where a typewriter has been set up. My teacher is Mrs. Hudson, a kind, gravelly voiced woman whose husband owns a dairy farm.

The room smells of old army blankets. We sit hunched over a Royal typewriter, and I press my chin to the cold metal hood of the machine, absorbing its intricate smells of rubber and grease. Even the ribbon has a smell, a starchy scent like the collar of an exotic shirt. Years later, when I went to Guiding Eyes for the

Blind, I was shown the typing room. At Guiding Eyes everything was up to date, there were talking IBM computers and wonderful LaserJet printers that could print out in ink or braille. But there in a corner were the old typewriters. I pictured them in a jungle of impossible lushness with howler monkeys hanging down over the heads of blind typists.

I quickly grow to love the typing hour each morning. My fingers are fast, and my hands race over the keyboard like carpenter bees exploring a trellis. Mrs. Hudson declaims the logarithmic poetry of her typing manual with a kind of flourish as my speed grows to sixty words per minute. Soon I am left to writing stories while Mrs. Hudson and the nurse drink coffee. Because I'd been reading Kipling on records, I fashion a primeval forest and fill it with conversational birds. Sometimes I write about submarines, sinking ships, people lost at sea.

At home typing becomes an exclusive activity, and I picture myself writing a novel about men in the Pacific fighting the Japanese. In the mornings, with Mrs. Hudson, I return to my Scandinavian themes. A farm girl goes to the well and strikes a troll with her bucket. He pulls her into his cavern, which is filled with yellow, sweet-scented violets. He has animals—birds and goats and so forth—and these animals talk, mostly about the great braininess of the troll. The girl notices that the troll has no mirrors.

I once had the opportunity to spend time with an Argentine man whose mother walked every day with Jorge Luis Borges, the blind poet who lived in Buenos Aires. Each day Borges, according to the story, would walk with his woman friend through a great arcade. As they strolled, Borges would narrate what he was seeing: a carnival filled with birds and lovely creatures. He told funny, involuted, decorous stories about the world that he could invent as a means of navigating the hours. The stories were an amusement, the intellectual equivalent of card playing, a pictorial solitaire that could be shared, a demarcation of art and of mental health.

Much later I would read the diaries of nineteenth-century "patients" in the first American institutions for the blind. Mary Day was grateful for her music lessons: they gave her the means to shape her blindness, her days could become a tapestry of sounds. How boring it must have been to converse with the bloodless minister who made the rounds of the Blind Asylum. I imagined those dreaded conversations without shape, their sole purpose to endlessly affirm that God has a plan for you.

Closed against boyhood with a typewriter, talking books and a radio is largely how I survive. I work the keys, hear the words, and spin the dials with no one to witness me. There is freedom in static! I discover the shortwave bands, the ocean of restless sound. There are winds out there, ships, and voices making their appointed rounds.

Spinning the dial, I hear the sharp, burning rose of Syrian love songs, the music of Turkistan.

I picture bright-edged clouds crossing the moon. Here there is clarity. In the radio light I see everything.

Auden wrote: "Thousands have lived without love, none without water."

Water arrives in so many forms. Enrico Caruso took Helen Keller gently by the hand and placed her electrically sensitive fingertips against his throat. He sang for her, *"Vois ma misère, hélas! Vois ma détresse!"* the aria from Saint-Saëns's *Samson et Dalila,* in which Samson laments his loss of sight. The great tenor sang in full voice, guiding her fingertips over his legendary vocal cords.

Imagine placing your hands delicately on a living hive.

· · ·

IT'S APRIL AND very cold. My grandmother is airing out her house, a long-in-the-tooth yellow Victorian. The New England spring is still over the next hill. My grandmother, Boston Irish, a chain smoker, holds on to this multistoried remnant of the town's prosperous era. Her husband had been a munitions expert, a manufacturer of mortar shells. He was one of the first Americans to build motorcycles. His eccentric taste still rules the house: a taxidermied fish sticks out three-dimensionally from a picture frame. Next to this is a photograph of Geraldine Farrar, star soprano of the Metropolitan Opera, circa 1916. Inside an unused fireplace is the stuffed head of a moose. The moose, in turn, is wearing a monocle. For some reason there are Lebanese worry beads hanging from its antlers. On either side of the hearth-moose are blackened iron Hessian soldiers—they once held logs in place. Above the mantel is a stipple-and-crayon engraving of some romantic beauty. Having climbed on a tall chair and hoisted myself up to put my nose right on her, I know she's there.

I'm playing hide-and-seek with my cousin Jim and my sister, Carol. We're roaming my grandmother's house. I am "it" and, wanting to rise to the challenge, I'm going to secrete myself in the attic of this four-story museum.

Push Vaseline into your eyes, then wander a strange house attempting to hide. You're in the great twelve-doored Golden Mosque trying not to make a sound. I can't see if I'm being seen, must rely on the ancient tribal trick of stepping on sticks without snapping them.

Up a curving stairwell I go, up and then up again, until I've reached the attic. Jim and Carol don't like it here: it's a place of ghosts.

Even in the attic there are rooms and more rooms. A raccoon coat hangs in a doorway, a huge anthropoid black ghastliness stopping my breath until I inch forward and touch it. Dead moths fall like specks of tissue paper. There's a smell of spoiled rubber, and then I find them under the hanging coats, a pair of gutta-percha boots, the height of two umbrella stands. Inside the left one is a rolled newspaper, and inside the paper is a pair of broken horn-rimmed glasses, a memento of a fishing trip.

In the next room is a rough bench with the parts of several machines, springs, gears, the coiled electric magnet of a radio. How weird these things are when you put them against your eye for verification. Even pressed against my face, the objects are indistinct as night trees. (Why do scraps of old machines smell like incense?)

In 1914 the house had burned, and charred keepsakes still remain: a wall clock, its wooden case scarred from heat. There is soot on its face and in the gears. And here's a burned gaming table, something with tall wooden sides like gunwales. I don't know what the game might have been—did it require a ball or a spinning top? My fingers find compartments, raised numbers.

There are doors in the attic that open into the deepest closets, places of rich concealment, rooms without lights, rooms that have never had lights. In here I am not at a disadvantage: my body is like a falling silk scarf in the blackness.

This is a treasury, and I open it: the attic closet is my *sebeel*, my Mohammedan drinking chamber.

There are trunks here, steamer trunks with rivets and leather straps, and inside them are smaller boxes—they open like Russian dolls, inside are smaller dolls, until you finally hold a bead in your fingers. My hands are actually breathing. This is pleasure: to be blind in the museum dark, unwrapping and holding.

I'll never be found here. By now my sister and cousin have given up looking and have traipsed outside. From the top of the house I can hear them far below, playing baseball in the yard.

■ ■ ■

MY DAYLIGHT WORLD is all too often a rude awakening. On the school playground, loitering on the sidelines, I rub my eyes in the terrible light. There are fast-moving pastels—a softball game is in progress. The gym teacher doesn't want me in the game, but I am expected to stand there as if the fresh air alone were a substitute for physical education.

My head is filled with Radio Norway. Peer Gynt is sailing in the night. There is a roaring and bellowing of trolls.

Someone calls suddenly: my help is needed!

"Hey, Crisco! Fat in a can! Throw me that glove!"

I am standing on a baseball mitt, but I'm solidly in the house of the troll.

The truth is, I *am* fat. In the privacy of my room, I have been eating like Elvis Presley, sponging up the clabber, swallowing great gobs of cookies and ice cream. With no exercise plan, I've ballooned. By the fourth grade, I am buried in my girth, fat with anguish and defeat.

In the school's dark hallways I am far too actual, pushed into the metal walls of lockers by bullies. I am their pastime.

"Blindo! You gross fucker!"

"He fucks his sister!"

I'm shoved in the back while climbing stairs.

I'm dragged from invisibility.

One day after gym I'm forced to shower with my enemies, though I've had no exercise. My tormentors' eyes fasten on my nakedness.

"Look at his prick! Look at his prick!"

"It looks like a milk bottle!"

(I am uncircumcised.)

I make my way with my hands outstretched.

"Milk bottle! Milk bottle!"

Again my glasses are stolen.

I want only to escape into the dark once more.

At night I sit in the heavy vigil of personal confinement. I eat alone in my room. In my obscure corner I brood over my ugliness. I am a green and distorted mass. My eyes dart about in my head. Who wouldn't laugh? This is my face, blubbering, cross-eyed.

Here come the villagers with their blazing torches, pursuing the Frankenstein monster to the ruined castle.

Small wonder that I love the attic and the enormous barn where my uncle keeps his dry-docked cabin cruiser. My cousin Jim points me to the rickety apple ladder that leans against the boat's hull, and one by one we climb into the pilot's cabin. Jim is, along with my sister, my true camarado, and we spend hours pursuing intricate fantasies aboard this boat. With hindsight, I understand that Jim was a lonely kid too. Always too big for his age and often falling short of his parents' expectations, he was ready to play in whatever dusty corner we could find.

The twilight is at the barn door. A white owl lives there in the rafters, and we can hear him scrambling. Far below us the barn cats circle our boat, manatees, sharks, narwhals. . . .

We're heading out of Singapore or Reykjavík, some radio name, Porta Capuana, Toulouse. My vistas are furnished by the shortwave and the talking books I've listened to.

I'm at the mahogany wheel, one of my uncle's cellophane-wrapped cigars in my teeth.

"Jim," I shout, "here comes the hail!"

"Aye-aye sir!" Jim is a good sport, answering, reorganizing possibilities. "There's a sail, captain!"

Together we see the white exploding glimmer of approaching sails as the air chills.

"Aye, the air is bracing!" I've acquired *bracing* from the Hardy Boys books, along with *crestfallen*.

"They've put out a lifeboat, sir!"

"Hard to starboard!"

"It's the women and children!"

"The infernal redcoats! They've hit her below the waterline!"

"Their ship's going down, Jim! We mustn't get too close, the suction will drag us down!"

We lean against the windows, pull throttles, scream in recognition of drowning humanity, their lifeboats going down with their ship. Afterward we clamber down the apple ladder and pretend to be divers, motioning with our arms, exploring the sunken staterooms. We clutch sticks, ready to do battle with barracuda.

Beyond the barn the night has become final, lights are on in the houses.

4

—

MY MOTHER, BLESS her, starts seeing ghosts. She is brittle, physically changed by accidents, bad falls on the stairs, minor auto scrapes. In the span of a few short years she has had surgery on her neck, elbows, shoulders, knees. She leans like a gondolier who has stepped onshore. She begins imagining, much as the poet Yeats did, that the dead are avid to share their visions and that no empty room is ever really empty. My mother walks with a cane, wears a sling, takes painkillers, reads books by Edgar Cayce. Our house has many drawn curtains, much clutter.

I remember my mother saying that she thought she was hanged for horse thievery in a prior life, because to this day she couldn't wear turtlenecks.

She's up all night reading about dead souls. There is spilled Scotch on the kitchen table.

Sometimes owing to a sinus infection, she appears wearing a

burnoose over her face. A peppermint smell is perceptible in all the rooms through which she has walked.

She is unhappy and beautifully eccentric, a suburban woman whose private deities are tattered like dolls one might find at the Salvation Army. "There are those," writes Kenneth Rexroth, "who spend all their lives / Whirling in love and hate / Of the deities they create."

My mother sees ghosts while my sister and I are at school. When we come home, she describes apparitions that have flickered at the tops of stairwells, a man in a black coat who stood in a doorway for a split second. She loves these contingent creatures; the ghosts are like small-town librarians moving past windows in the pale green moonlight. We had all sorts of odd conversations which today I can't recall exactly, but they often went something like this:

"I saw the man with the hat today," she might say, meeting us in the yard.

"What was he doing?" My sister is scuffing her shoes—it's as if we were discussing what's for supper.

"I only caught him for a second, he was passing through the living-room doorway. He jumps a little as he walks."

"Like Charlie Chaplin?" I've seen Chaplin by pressing my nose on the TV screen. To my eye, he looks like a frenzied hen, or a hen shadow, something not precisely in the shape of a man.

"He's more like the German Kaiser."

My mother lives with her ghosts the way some live with nervous stimulants. This requires many trips to the library for more material on the occult. We climb into the station wagon after school and pull out of the garage in the red sunlight, the car lurching backward in bursts. My mother drives like a novitiate—and in the vastness of the gold fog that is my seeing, these car trips are more terrible than the haunted house. The long blue miles to the library are a roller coaster in the beat-up Chevrolet.

Riding in a car with a bad driver requires trust and faith. When you're blind, the insecure driver is a human transmitter, the palpable radio frequencies of poor road handling flicker inside us, the wedding of light and darkness, road and metal, passes right through the fillings in our teeth. Through the car's windows I see a measureless layer cake of gray strata, wild lights, a relentless surf. And my mother is all over the road. The tension in the car rises like air forced from a vacuum pump, and then suddenly with a bump we're in the library's parking lot, the brakes catching and releasing a dozen times before we come to a stop.

During these rides I imagine the dead floating along above the car, riding on Persian rugs. The spirits are sailing back to the library to sleep in the books as vampires do inside their coffins.

In the reading room I'm too self-conscious to put my nose against an open page, and so I walk the aisles, where it smells of acidic paper and wood. The spines of books wave like strands of kelp; there are abalone shells and geodes on the shelves.

Apparitions only become ghosts when no one can explain them. Sir Walter Scott thought he'd seen the ghost of Byron until he looked more closely and saw it was a cloak hanging from a hook. My eyes are engines of apparition—the wild cyclamen grows straight across my iris, puts out leaves over my pupil.

I have no ghosts in my head.

But for my mother the dead are like Nijinsky: they jump from the soiled drabs of her repressions. Ghosts are possibility seen backward: no one is blind, the world is etherealized, nothing has to be dark or final.

Often she sits up all night. I can hear her moving around downstairs, the clatter of dishes, closets opened and closed. Occasionally I investigate, and even though it's two A.M., she reads to me from Bram Stoker's *Dracula* or something about shipwrecks. The *Lusitania*, *Titanic*, *Andrea Doria*, the *Hindenburg*, the failed arctic expeditions. We read about dying people in the middle of the night.

The Russian poet Aleksander Blok had a vision of reincarnation: he was destined to return in life-after-life to the same cold street corner where, in the middle of the night, there is only a streetlamp and the illuminated window of a drugstore. Just so, I would fear returning to those car rides, the midnight sofa. My mother, gloomy, reading.

My father never sees ghosts. He's a reader of *The New York Times*, a Harvard Ph.D. with depths of Finnish pragmatism. Because I never discuss my blindness, he's content to view me as sighted. He is a man who believes in mind over matter. He likes simple meals, bread and cheese, instant coffee. My mother's emergent frailty and odd sleep patterns do not seem to faze him: he makes his toast, reads the *Times*, listens to E. Power Biggs on the radio. He seems uncomfortable in the world of physical realities, hates doing anything that involves the use of tools, even hanging a picture can frustrate him. He likes his books, lives in print.

When I am in third grade, we move from rural New Hampshire to a suburban enclave in Albany, where my father has taken a government job in state education. At dusk he takes walks with our family dog, a golden retriever, and now and then I tag along, peering into the twilight through the dirty windows of my hopeless glasses. I walk briskly, picking up my feet like a soldier, aware that this keeps me from tripping over unexpected rises in the pavement. I'm always having to anticipate what might happen, like a fisherman in mist, wading in the river's shallows.

We talk, playing an alphabet game, the sentences suggested by each letter.

I begin: "Always an abacus arranges arithmetic."

"Before beads bring boredom."

"Creating certain circus cravings."

"Defeating determination!"

"Excitement entreats everyone!"

"Fools forget figures!"

"Geometry goes gaga!"

My appetite for seeing is fed by lingo as vanilla.

I had long been turning pages and listening to recorded books on a hundred green afternoons that turned to evening without invasion. I listened to books from the Library of Congress for whole days at a stretch, sometimes feigning illness to stay home from school and while away the hours with *Life on the Mississippi* or *Huckleberry Finn*.

Now, thirty years later, friends ask how I know so many lines of text by heart. Even as a boy among the rough-and-tumble kids of rural New Hampshire, I was known as "the walking dictionary."

I stayed alone in rooms, listening as a daily ritual, hardening my memory, making my tongue sharp.

Blind Darwin, his *Beagle* the recorded book.

I'm knee-deep in the private fireflies, the ones inside my eyes. The night moves against my face like a drowsy hand.

My father and I walk for an hour, and I talk about anything, grapes of the Loire, *The Grapes of Wrath*. . . .

Why can't I tell him how little I'm seeing? What's wrong with a life of color and light, inferences pouring through my skin like dream-water?

How do you personalize darkness, make it yours, if you're living in denial? I have no affection for my life, must talk, impress my father, become a being of value.

I thrived on suborning my blindness. My parents were perfect accomplices, loving, eccentric, well-meaning, dotty.

I walk bent forward, shoveling words into life's furnace. I am not lost.

■ ■ ■

THE CRAVING TO appear like your peers is an enslavement at any age, but it is particularly bad in childhood, and it only gets worse in adolescence. Add to this the excitement of passing as a sighted person, the exhilaration of walking the top of a steep fence without falling. Standing on weakened chairs to reach a top shelf is a primeval joy. Imagine that your every minute is constructed from small or large sequential risks.

Like John Metcalf, the nineteenth-century British architect and road builder, I keep my blindness as a private puzzle. Metcalf was so vigorous in his daily walks that strangers never guessed his blindness. I can't pretend that I am completely successful. Frequently I am singled out for derision, but the addiction to pass is stronger with every instance of humiliation.

My success, such as it is, depends on an array of acquired and practiced skills. I possess tremendous hand-to-eye coordination: if I know that a football is being thrown my way, I can often catch it. Landscapes, streets, the timbre of voices, the location of furniture, the exact placement of even the smallest objects in a room, are imprinted and revised almost hourly.

It is the unfamiliar or the unexpected that can catch me, and when it does, I find that with a little vaudeville shambling, I can appear merely confused. Everyone walks into a coatrack or a closet—at least now and then. (Charlie Chaplin turned this into a science.) I begin this eccentric waltz with my mother's own fears that blindness means a reduced life for her child. But behind every facsimile of accomplishment lies that word, like a corset with a thousand minute laces, each one a thread of normalcy.

On Lake Winnepesaukee, where my parents own a cottage, I insist on driving our family's power boat. I insist on this throughout my childhood. My parents are uncomfortable with the boat, having never mastered docking it, mooring it, or snapping down the canvas. For them the boat is a necessary evil—our cottage is on an island—but to me the boat is everything, the pure "objective correlative" of my hunger for normalcy. I must drive it. So my father sits next to me, narrating our course down the center of the waterway, steering me a little to the left or right as oncoming boats are sighted.

Sometimes my father says, "Can you see that breakwater over there? Aim to the left of it." But I can never see what he's talking about. I just aim the bow and hit the throttle.

I'm terrified.

But shit, driving the boat, I'm not caught between warring snakes of definition: blind I'm a fatted failure; posing as a sighted person, I'm on a terrible high-wire.

But people will only like me if I can see.

The wide intervals of lake draw me forward, and I *will* drive the boat.

In the meantime I'm a tired kid. It's preposterous to live as though you can see. Looking back, I can scarcely imagine the energy it took.

Back in the schoolroom, I get tangled up in my body. In math class I raise my hand, ask a question, trying to stay on the same ocean with the others.

"Who are you talking to?" says the math teacher, a very young woman, a girl really. Someone whose gaze can make me blush.

"Your eyes don't look right at me," she says.

Now the class is laughing.

"I don't know who you're talking to," she says.

The laughter is a calliope, steam driven.

All my teachers know I'm blind. After school, in the twilight, I must go for extra help. Must have the math problems explained over and over.

Now I stand up, knocking over my chair in haste, reeling for the door.

More laughter.

I stumble into the hallway like a child who has wet his pants.

For refuge I have the nurse's office, where I lie in the dark like Tutankhamen. My mask is a cold cloth.

There are headaches that spread from my skull to my stomach. My entire body is uninhabitable. I have backaches from leaning and straining to see.

The heat inside my body is oppressive: I'm parched, clogged. Never have I been so thirsty.

Today I wonder if John Metcalf ever felt this way, hiding from his blindness, tramping the British moors. Was he thirsty? Did he experience nausea too?

. . .

GREEN IS GREEN, and I am falling through the spring of my thirteenth year. In my early teens my eyes begin to hurt almost continuously. The eyes don't cross, but neither do they stay straight. I take Fiorinal tablets, Darvon, aspirin with codeine.

My brain is singing madly.

My mother, who suffers from a hundred maladies, believes me when I tell her I'm too ill to leave the house. As luck would have it, I actually develop a case of mononucleosis and miss seven months of school.

My glossy brain flares like sunspots.

Sometimes during the day while my mother sleeps, I drink beer from the refrigerator.

I sit with my face pressed to the television's glass tube and listen to game shows.

I eat enormous cans of potato chips, whole boxes of cookies, entire cheeses, bins of plums, peaches.

This is eating without volition, architectural eating, tastes buttressing the dense spirit.

I wander the house and press my nose into every crevice. Of particular interest are books on the French Revolution that have ink drawings of the guillotine, the executioners holding decapitated heads by the hair. And the tortured faces of those still waiting in the tumbrel! My peachy face is jammed into the very crotch of the book. My eyes are leaping like the sparks in a monster movie, but I am fastening on these gruesome pictures with absolute attention.

The four o'clock movie is often disasters or wars. I can't get enough of the sinking ships, the men trapped in submarines, the *Titanic* going down. I'm a fat little Roman in love with vicarious suffering. With my mouth full of chocolate, I contemplate the dying passengers. I love the sounds of disaster coming through the tissue-thin speakers of the TV.

Outside, the sun is going down, kids are playing, cars crunch gravel. But I am released, unseen, thriving on shrieks.

I am also more than a little stoned: glued together on Darvon, chocolate chips, bleu cheese straight from the foil. My flesh weighs me down like a rude sack of potatoes. I'm shaped like a petty burgher in a Daumier sketch.

Now and then when the planets are right, my mother takes me shopping. We must go to stores with names like Husky Boys, where I try on stiff corduroy pants, pulling them high over my fleshpale stomach.

In the attic, with wind at the eaves, I push my one usable eye deep into the lingerie pages of a Sears catalog and masturbate into a T-shirt.

I do it breathlessly, nose to page, down on my hands and knees. Blind Portnoy!

This is what girls look like! Look at this! It's perfection! Curve of breasts, hair cascading!

My God!

I'm Quasimodo.

Who would ever accept my passionate approach?

How will I ever get close enough to see a girl's face?

Each morning now a woman comes to our house, sent by the school district. She bends forward with her horn-rimmed glasses perched on her nose, as if by putting her face next to mine, I will see the impossible page. Her hands are terribly red. Her breath smells of coffee.

I know that no real girl will ever come this close.

I'm knotted, freakish, my bowels are full of gas.

I bend, contorted, concentrating on numbers. But straining to solve the math problem, I know how lamentable I am. The radius of a circle is the sun itself, the eye that watches me.

After the teacher leaves and my mother has gone back to sleep, I go outside, where I'm as white and fat as the Dowager Empress of China.

5

—

IN MAY OF 1970 my father decides to take a job as the president of Hobart and William Smith Colleges, two tiny liberal arts schools in Geneva, New York. He describes the campus as a cluster of old crumbling buildings that are situated on a hillside overlooking Seneca Lake. The place, he says, has an aura of genteel shabbiness—and he's right.

The president's house, where we'll be living, is a drafty Greek Revival affair that shudders when trucks pass. The decorative columns are full of insects, the walls in the cellar are crumbling into red dust. You can hear the house settle; the windows vibrate.

At the local historical society there's a file about the house. During the First World War it was used as a military clinic. Wounded troops were quartered in every room. I picture them in high beds with tiny flags beside them, their arms tattooed with roses and women. At night when I lie down in this haunted chamber, my hair smells of smoke and incense. There are squirrels in the walls.

On the second floor deep in the rear, there's an octagonal room that was designed for séances. This region of New York was famous in the 1880s for its tea party conversations with the dead. The founder of the local college saw the victims of shipwrecks in this room, saw Aristotle, saw a quivering fire shaped like a woman. He imagined wheels revolving in the heavens, much as Yeats did with his gyres.

What could be better than dreaming in such a room? I push my face into books of photographs that I've borrowed from the college library. In one, a dozen blind men sit at a table in a coffee warehouse. It's 1885, the gilded age. There's something grand about American progress: a palpable thing transmitted by telephone and electric light. American railway stations are loftier than all the palaces of Europe. Even a coffee warehouse in Manhattan arches like a cathedral. Sunlight from its windows falls in long shafts through the vault, catching the blind men at their table. They look as if they might be sitting in Barnum's center ring, a novelty, twelve blind men drinking coffee.

The men are shown in varying aspects of consideration, with heads tilted up or down or slightly to the side, as if a confidence were about to be shared with the empty air. Theirs is the hypnagogic state between waking and sleep that fascinated Edgar Allan Poe. Even in this temple of American progress the faces of the blind excite the greatest degree of superstition: these men raise their cups of coffee like Tiresias the prophet, who was blinded by Hera, then compensated by Zeus with the gift of soothsaying.

It is common to believe the blind have occult powers. In the

Midrash it says, "The Lord opens the eyes of the blind." In ancient Israel the blind were legendary for their feats of memory, many of them recalling whole books on command. The learned blind were known as "baskets of books." They were vessels, these figures, and legends say that they were infused with prayerful intensities. They became templars, priests of a gnostic society known to Charon. Their one talent was their compensatory payment from God—all human feats of memory or articulation became the proof of a divine intervention. As a result, the blind have appeared throughout history as bearers of divine judgment. Therefore the blind are to be taken with all seriousness: the earliest schools for the blind were devised by Egyptian priests. The coffee drinkers are descended from a vast and powerful clan.

The blind muezzin climbs the parapet and sings at dawn. The shaman in Lapland is depicted as a blind man: for days at a time his soul leaves his body and travels under the earth, moving through the viscera of his buried ancestors. The living body of the shaman sits upright, blind to the light. Everywhere in the world's legends one finds blind sorcerers. Blindness is a natural coefficient of magic. Sometimes blindness is the result of malevolent punishments, as sorcerers have been known to blind men and women without warning. This sudden blindness that comes from the heavens is the oldest source of superstition. In the ancient world blindness was most often thought to be a calamity.

In my sorcerer's room I imagine the tomb of the unknown blind. There are the children of Sparta, each encased in the small earthenware tub that the ancients used as vessels of euthanasia. Picture row upon row of blind infants in their clay shells lying on the hills under the moon.

Now come the blind at the temples of Epidaurus, all of them

persuaded that they can see after a night of inhaling the Egyptian vapors.

The beggars of Rome are here, their eyes put out for villainous offenses. Here as well are the blind Roman prostitutes.

Eratosthenes the scholar is here: according to Euripides, he starved himself to death as his blindness began.

Here are the medieval blind of Paris, veterans of the Crusades. They formed a religious order, wore long blue robes with a distinctive lily on each breast, and observed their secret rites.

Here are the street fiddlers, lottery sellers, broom makers, basket menders; the centuries of the blind accompanied by untrained dogs. Here are the rhapsodes and singers from ancient Israel and India; the blind storytellers in the woods of Finland.

Here is Blind Tom the "marvelous prodigy"—a slave child from the Confederacy who played the piano by ear. Imagine the notes from a damp and poorly tuned instrument in a great house in Charleston.

Here is Didymus, the Alexandrian scholar; Nicholas Saunderson, the eighteenth-century Cambridge mathematician; Blind Jacob of Netra, a Hessian German of the eighteenth century who fashioned a system of reading using notched sticks.

Here is the blind man of Puisaux, who told the philosopher Diderot that aside from sight, he would like to have long arms—he might then investigate the moon.

■ ■ ■

MY MOTHER, OF course, continues to see ghosts. They may reappear to her at any time of day or night. Her life is complicated by misplaced objects: hairbrushes, car keys, notebooks, all of which she believes have been spirited throughout the house by poltergeists. Unable to sleep at night, she spends her daylight hours on the long velour sofa in the drawing room. Because she takes many painkillers, she's in her own hypnagogic state. Her ghosts are quite real; I understand this even as a teenager.

My father and I watch Walter Cronkite together and take long walks in the night, talking about the Vietnam War, the disasters of Nixon. With him for company, I learn the streets of the town, the quadrangles. By day I will walk solo, holding my head up. Passing.

As a teenager, I flew in my skull and longed to be able to flirt; to see in a girl some kind of notice. Still, desire is conveyed by a fixed eye. The steady eye makes one available, places us in the center of a room. But my eyes would not hold still: they went in all directions like the seeds of thistles. How would I get from the curtained room to the open light? My high-school yearbook shows me without glasses, staring at the photographer as through a fish tank. My eyes are a wound in the center of my face. My mouth is slack, as if I'd awakened from a dream I can't fully recall.

In the schoolroom my problems are legion. In science class, for example, we are making some kind of wind experiment. In pairs we build glass boxes into which wind will be introduced. Inside the boxes are stones, green plants, and a stalk of burning hemp. I forget exactly how it works—we're to see how the smoke rises or falls with changes in the atmosphere.

Lenny Marcus is my partner. He does most of the work while I talk. The experiment means nothing to me. It's merely visual.

"There's a castle just beyond sunrise where the dead live," I tell him. "It's a Gypsy story. The dead are all standing on their heads. Sometimes they stand up and slap each other, that's how they kiss."

Poor Lenny: he's hoping smoke will rise in a box.

"The Gypsies have carved bone horns, long whips, ride in carriages back and forth to the land of the dead. It takes five hundred years to equal one day in dead land. So of course the Gypsies never get back to their starting place."

Lenny's experiment is not going well. Smoke is escaping from the box. It smells like burning cork. But thank God for his efforts. Without his loyalty to seventh-grade science, I wouldn't have learned anything. As it is, I understand how fog sinks toward the earth.

I fail tests in biology because the print is faintly mimeographed and far too small; I'm barred from sports; I'm ridiculed by a chemistry teacher who sees me whispering to the boy next to me. I'm asking for blackboard elaboration, but the teacher announces that "we must have something special going on."

■ ■ ■

I BEGIN MINING my hunger.

In the attic, in all the fractions of denial, I'm growing thinner.

I conjure tutelary angels, seraphs who will spin me faster, burning my incompleteness into blackened sugar. My flesh is beginning to burn, the leaves and bark of my viscera flaring in unison with my mad eyes.

My guts have started to smolder.

It's a beautiful thing: a wild descent into the purifying intra-intestinal fires.

I'm learning how to starve.

Evenings I excuse myself from supper and climb to the attic, where I hunch into the rustlings, a silvery, voracious fuse.

I tell my parents I have a stomachache, and I do. I'm overflowing with blind shame, embarrassments of the flesh, humiliation of the demiurge: I cannot look you in the eye. In the mornings I drink only coffee. At noon in the high school's cafeteria I permit myself one brownie and a carton of milk.

At home, what with the accumulations of Kent State, Cambodia, a pending campuswide moratorium, dinner recedes like a tidal shelf. We no longer gather at set times. The air is fuzzy with Scotch whiskey and cigarettes as faculty and administrators wrestle with the problems of the week. The larger politics are monolithic; the sink fills with cups.

I am free to go without, and in the attic I listen to the Velvet Underground through headphones. I plan to be urgent and skeletal like John Lennon or Lou Reed. The hunger is laved in speed and song. I press my nose to the cardboard album covers, admiring the sunless faces of the Rolling Stones. Each grins from a cloud and is thin as Christ.

At first there is power in this. I'm watched in a new way. Weight is vanishing, and no one looks at my face. My identity is being solicitously honed.

My looking glass becomes hashish. I am Narcissus with hemp, I spin in Augustinian depression. At seventeen I discover stories about the street urchins of Marrakesh who are paralyzed by oceanic chords of light, waves of glory. They smoke and lie down, and rats nibble on their ears.

If I can't effectually see anyone, I may as well make a cult of it.

I anathematize the school, the teachers, the frenzy of sports. To be touched somehow, my true goal, is years ahead of me. Still, I begin to have some friends, all of them soured because the actual world is covered by an indescribable stain. Each climbs his own lookout tower, quick, disheveled, obscure. We're all waiting for the silver ship to arrive, a paradise of fruit, the Beloved from the Song of Solomon, merciful nights among the hazel trees.

Nights we meet in the snowy public park with bottles of

cherry brandy in our coats, then walk down to the lake. There, under the elevated highway, we smoke pot. All of us are lost in the nacreous haze. I discover the fitfully lit places of the underage drinker and pot smoker, the little cracked door at the municipal water-pumping station where on snowy nights we can light our matches.

We ride in a Dodge Dart burning holes in our shirts. By spring there's a marked aroma, jasmine and honeysuckle, in the pipe. Delirium of flowers and charcoal.

To be in this company, I'll master my terror of automobiles. There's a thread of honey and wire that runs up my spine. The car bounces over a bridge, then takes a left, bumps down a dirt path to the canal, comes to rest in high weeds. Somewhere a night train crosses a trestle. We're laughing, falling, tumbling out of the car, each of us waving his invisible shining branch.

Darrell is an orphan. His adoptive parents are prominent in town. His surrogate father is red-faced, upper middle class, a big game hunter when he takes vacations. Darrell never goes on these junkets—he stays home with his older sister. Together they raid their father's liquor cabinets. At the canal's edge he waves a bottle of Chivas Regal in the air like a bandit.

"They're fucked," he says. He points to people fishing in a skiff floating about a half mile away.

"These fish are just cancer on a stick!"

There's a nuclear plant upcanal, a famous one.

"Eat shit!"

"Eat this!"

Smoke. Laughter. We're fog colored. We're sitting in a nest of weeds.

The insects are rising, river mosquitoes.

Sandy blows smoke, coughs, says something about bats.

"Yeah, they eat six hundred mosquitoes an hour." Bill is a reader. His father's an air force colonel. Bill thinks his father hates him, shrouds him in endless accusations.

Darrell: "I caught a bat in the garage. Nailed that fucker right to the door. Crucified it."

"Was it alive?"

"Of course it was alive, you can't crucify something dead!"

A glass pipe goes around, coals glowing at one end.

I begin reciting: " 'Fillet of a fenny snake / In the cauldron boil and bake: / Eye of newt and toe of frog, / Wool of bat and tongue of dog . . .' "

Darrell joins in: " 'For a charm of powerful trouble, / Like a hell-broth boil and bubble!' "

He leaps into the canal. He keeps his pants on, to guard against theft.

But no one in this group would steal his clothes. He's too cool, too good looking. He's the only one in the group of four school-boys who's been laid. He has more than a hint of sadism, he's all voice and blood. Swimming in the canal without a word, he dives.

Under the dripping trees I finger the gold capsule of a ciga-rette lighter, rub my naked foot on a stone. The drugs bring up paranoia, and for a blind kid there's no visual check, no way to confirm or deny the dangers.

There's a crunch of gravel from the far side of the canal. Suddenly there's a flashlight beam from the woods. "It's a cop!"

Darrell is still underwater. Everyone scrambles, separate beings now, the bloody gout of not seeing hangs before each of us as we run.

In the undergrowth are the ruins of outdoor cooking grills, remnants of the days when the state maintained the park.

There's a howl as someone stumbles into one of these, then a silence. Bill has badly bruised his leg on a cement fireplace. Darrell laughs from the canal, splashes water in all directions.

There are no cops.

"It was the rowboat," he yells. "They're going home to eat the cancer fish!"

. . .

I MUST SLEEP with the electric blanket on high. I've dropped below 105 pounds.

My mother begins to be alarmed. For a while my emergent thinness is praiseworthy, I've been remade, I look convincingly refreshed. I seem to have some friends. But now it's clear I'm not eating.

She sits me down at our kitchen table, puts before me a steak, some potatoes, beans. I refuse to eat, telling her my guts hurt, telling her there must be something wrong. I try to soften the blow.

Upstairs I'm free to be urgently thin, inverted around my disappearance. My shrinking is an abstraction, just as I am. Together we are a species. Down to bones, we're at the height of our strength.

I want to be thinner. There's no eloquence to it.

"My guts hurt" is all I can say.

The family doctor probes, orders tests: X rays, and an upper GI series that involves the drinking of barium.

In my hospital gown I'm exactly 100 pounds. My ribs are terrible to see, there's hardly any flesh. My hips stand out like ears.

I press my prick and sternum against a metal tray, and photographs are taken.

"My guts hurt," I tell them again. "I don't really need to eat."

They order the "lower GI series," X rays that require a barium enema.

In bed, grotesquely on my side, gown open, a young girl hardly older than I am bends to give me the enema. I'm burning with disgrace, imagining her giggling with friends after dark.

Then I must hold it in. I sit on my rank haunches. The nurse gives me permission to let go, and sailing into the dying infancy of anorexia, I let go.

Next, in another test, meat is fed down my gullet on a string, my eyes wide open, my face raving with indignity.

On the cusp of dying I have achieved a figure.

I believe I'm beautiful.

I imagine that people will gravitate to me across the smoky room because I am the teenage Goya.

On my draft card I am five feet seven inches tall, my eyes are green, and I weigh 103 pounds. On the back it says that I'm ineligible for serving in the armed forces.

How inessential it is, this business of being loved. I'm smaller and smaller. Here are my naked wrists, almost clear.

Look how the world attends me.

Nurses bring me milk shakes, which I pour down the toilet. I'm a thirteenth-century novitiate practicing the *ars moriendi*, the holy art of dying.

Anorexia is a condition of puberty. Traumatized children resist the next stage: adulthood holds a future of steepened deformities.

Don't look at me. Look at me. Look.

By now I have a twenty-four-inch waist.

It's the midmoment of dying or living.

Amazing. The doctors shake their heads. All the tests prove that I am physiologically intact.

What's wrong with me?

Dear girl, I can't quite see you, come closer.

Don't I look like a sexy junkie?

■ ■ ■

OUR VOICES ARE slow. It's Halloween and very cold. We have cherry brandy and stolen wine. We're behind the abandoned Hotel Seneca in downtown Geneva. We're going to climb the fire escape, smoke reefer in the rooms. This is the castle at Arundel, we'll become earls the moment we possess it.

Up the building's flanks we go, then across a rotting windowsill. The place smells of coal and strawberries, a scent that I'll later find in eastern Europe under the linden trees in Berlin.

We drink the sulfuric wine and explode.

The moon appears to have broken the windows, that's how greedy it was to enter these rooms, to shine on bed springs, fractured picture frames. I'm wide open, a young king, owing no one an explanation, indifferent to blindness.

Some girl has left a garish kerchief on the floor; I find it when I sit down to smoke a cigarette. I lift it to my face. Red and gold.

All my internal mechanisms swim like fish. I imagine teen-age love-making in this place and wonder who else has been here.

The others want to put their burning hands on the world. They want to climb into a car, go roaring through the dirty farm towns, voyeuristic, cursing, hiccupping with laughter.

"I saw this chick blowing some guy right in front of a window!" says Darrell. "I almost drove off the fuckin' road!"

They climb down the fire escape, clamber into a car, and go

looking for trick-or-treaters whom they'll harass. I decide not to go with them and instead wander by the lakeshore.

. . .

ON A NIGHT of first snow I encounter Teddy and Moira by the fountain. They haven't seen me, they're necking, hands inside each other's coats. When I draw near, they don't seem at all irritated. It's as though the kissing will always go on, time is of no consequence.

"Check this out," Teddy says, and bends down to lift a metal plate. "It's the entry to the room under the fountain! Come on, we've got a flashlight!"

Down we go into the submarine, our shoes uncertain on the ladder's iron rungs.

Moira has raven hair, a long oval face, she looks a bit like the young Virginia Woolf. Teddy is round, bespectacled, Brillo-haired. He will become a first-rate jazz musician.

Down here, what with Moira's perfume and the dark earth, it smells like a Spanish church. The air is incredibly cold.

We are each seeking some kind of transparent nourishment. Moira wants to act. Teddy needs a town where he can play the horn. I'm under the roof of disability, an iron-colored room. I belong to fruitfulness but have no idea that blindness does too. It simply has not occurred to me that blindness is a rich way of living, rich as an oak tree or strong grapes.

I want to touch Moira's hair. In the subfountain temple she brushes against my cheek as she leans my way. She's floating toward my face, preparing to pass the reefer without letting any smoke escape from her mouth. Strands of her hair touch my ear, these are raven feathers, and I strain to see her with my wild pony eyes. And my lord she's gently touching my chin with her cold fingers—my first kiss, smoke passed ever so deftly into my mouth by a girl with jet-black hair.

I raise my hands as if they were clay pots. Behind my sternum Moira lights candles, each as cold as glass—now they are hot and thick.

Teddy is laughing.

Moira has moved against me, and now she leans toward Teddy, passing him the joint.

Under the fountain in this closet of machinery, no one can see me blushing. I'm a boy with a yellow crown, my hands are shaking. I can scarcely hold on to the flask of blackberry brandy.

The reefer has gone out. Teddy and Moira are giggling in the dark. Soon they will climb into Teddy's car and drive to a field somewhere and fuck with the heater on.

Much later I dream my mother knocks at my bedroom door. She's seen a ghost. She says it came right through the door of my room. It looked like a walking waterfall. She wonders if I saw it too.

I tell her that it looked like burning sulfur, a burst of green, a whip of fire. I see the faces of Moira and Teddy lit by match heads.

The ghost has vanished inside a wall.

All I want to do is drive, take Moira to the orchard, and there unfasten the tiny buttons on her blouse. I want to put my ear against her left breast, hear the heartbeats, kiss her fragrant white neck.

∎ ∎ ∎

MY FRIEND ARTHUR tells me that Mr. Morton, our eleventh-grade English teacher, has urged the class to pray for me. We're sitting under a thrilling summer night sky, the lake before us. We've taken LSD, a half tab apiece, and we've been walking all night in circuits. Arthur now sees what he thinks is the aurora borealis, northern lights, above the lake in shining curtains. He wants me to confirm it. I think of my mother and her ghosts, then tell him to look in tomorrow's newspaper.

"Why did Morton say the class should pray for me?"

Morton is a fine man, ill suited for teaching, in love with culture and God. Soon he will enter the ministry.

"He said no one knows what's wrong with you."

"That's all?"

"He said you might be dying."

"Did he say why?"

"He said you weigh only a hundred pounds, that you haven't been in school for a month. That you've been in the hospital. He said we should all pray for you."

I'm nervous from the acid, find myself pulling at hairs in my eyebrows.

"Well, did he say why I was dying?"

"No."

"Did anyone say anything?"

"No. No one said anything."

I'm trying to turn cards over inside my head, but I can't get my fingers around their edges.

"You mean no one laughed?"

"No one made a sound."

I wouldn't be telling the truth if I said that at that moment I regretted taking the acid. But I make a resolution that I should go to school. The teacher said the truth. I haven't been there in over a month. I've spent days roaming around like a sleeping wanderer. Blind Huck.

"Do you remember," I say to Arthur, "how Huck Finn tried

praying to see if God would give him a fishing pole? All he ever got was a bit of string."

I'm trying to imagine the power of prayer—other people's prayers. I don't quite get it, the connection between faith and reward in my life seems so far apart. But lately, I have been eating without appearing to have made a conscious choice. I don't know what changed me, but to this day, the Eucharist can start me weeping. "Take this bread and eat. This is my body."

Here is Jesus' richest gift, his spirit into bread.

6

I BELIEVE THAT in every blind person's imagination there are landscapes. The world is gray and marine blue, then a clump of brown shingled houses stands revealed by rays of sun, appearing now as bison—shaggy and still. These are the places learned by rote, their multiple effects of color made stranger by fast-moving clouds. The unknown is worse, an epic terrain that, in the mind's eye, could prevent a blind person from leaving home.

Since I know the miniature world of Geneva, New York, I decide to attend college there. On campus, though, there are sudden skateboards. I wish for a magic necklace to ward them away. The quadrangle is a world of predatory watching, and so I begin affecting a scowl. I look serious, as if my corpuscles have turned into hot pearls. I'm the angriest-looking boy on earth.

The dean's office knows about my eyes. I have a first-floor room in the dorm in case of fire. The theory is that with a vision impairment, I might not make it down the fire escape. This is the extent of the campus's support service for disabled students in 1973. The unreadable print in books, the dark dormitory room, the inaccessible library books—all these are things left to my dissemblings.

In the classroom I gravitate toward literature. The prevailing pedagogy is still centered on the New Criticism, a method of reading and analysis born in the years after World War II. This is a lucky break for me: the stress here is on the close reading of texts.

One simply has to read a poem to death.

The professor chain-smokes and takes the class line by line through turgid Victorian prosody. We crawl in the nicotine haze through the comma splices of Thomas Hardy.

I listen, hunched in my chair as the machinery of poets is dissected. We are eighteenth-century clock makers: nothing is too small for our rational little universe.

In the dim library I move through the stacks, pressing my nose to the spines. In my pocket I carry a letter from the eye doctor addressed "To Whom It May Concern"—it avows that too much reading is dangerous for me. "The scanning motions inherent in reading make retinal tearing more likely. Therefore Mr. Kuusisto should read in moderation."

Like all true talismans, this letter is frightening. It's designed to protect me from professors who may demand too much from me. But in my pocket it feels like a letter bomb.

Reading is hazardous!

And to me the words of poetry are onions, garlic, fennel, basil; the book itself an earthenware vessel.

Reading alone with a magnifying glass, nothing on earth makes more sense to me than Wallace Stevens's poem "The

Pleasures of Merely Circulating": "The angel flew round in the garden / the garden flew round with the clouds, / and the clouds flew around, and the clouds flew around, / and the clouds flew around with the clouds."

My spastic eye takes in every word like a red star seen on a winter night. Every syllable is acquired with pain. But poetry furnishes me with a lyric anger, and suddenly poems are wholly necessary. Robert Bly's book *The Light Around the Body,* for example, expresses an almost mystical combination of wonder and rage about "the Great Society." He depicts a world gone so awry that the very pine stumps start speaking of Goethe and Jesus, the insects dance, there are murdered kings in the light bulbs outside movie theaters. All of it is glorious, and like my boyhood discovery of Caruso in the attic, Bly's voice, among others—Breton, Nerval, Lorca—follows me in the dark.

■ ■ ■

I MOVE IN a solitude fueled by secrecy. O Lord, let me never be seen with the white cane. Let me roll through the heavy oceans like the beluga whale, filled with dark seeds, always coursing forward. Let no one find me out! This is my lacerating tune. Leaning over my private page, I shake with effort.

Weakness and *lack of affect* are the synonyms for the word *blind.* In Roget's Thesaurus one finds also: *ignorant, oblivious, obtuse, unaware, blocked, concealed, obstructed, hidden, illiterate, backward, crude, uneducated,* and worst of all, *unversed.*

At twilight I walk in the botanical gardens, the night smells richly of lilac. I've read that Immanuel Kant could not bear to visit his friends in sickness; after they died, he would repress all memories of them. There are limits to cognition and reason.

What would he think in the mad purple twilight where I live. Would he visit himself?

I hear radios and TV sets from the open windows on campus.

Under the violet streetlights my glasses, thick as dishes, fill with aberrations at the edges of their thick curves.

College is brutally difficult for me. One poem must take the place of the bulky novel I cannot read, or at least not read in a week. I often go home from the library with the few words I've been able to see and absorb still vivid in my imagination. Alone, I take the words apart and rearrange them like Marcel Duchamp playing chess with his own private rules. Still, I need extra time for every assignment. But exploring what words can do when placed side by side, I'm starting to build the instrument that will turn my blindness into a manner of seeing.

Still, walking around, feigning sight, I step in the rain-washed gutter, brush the street sign, and make a hundred slapstick gestures. In a flash I'm Stan Laurel, the angel of nutty innocence. This can happen without warning. It might be the telephone that does it. A friend calls, saying she'll meet me downstairs in half an hour. She drives a red Chrysler.

I walk down to the street and approach the car. I reach for the door on the passenger's side and give it a tug, but it's locked. I rap on the window, but my friend doesn't seem to hear. I rap again, tug on the door, rap and tug. Then I walk around to her side of the car. Is she in some Wagnerian trance, Brünnhilde at the wheel? When I lean down to her window, I see at last the face of a genuinely terrified Chinese woman. I motion to her to roll down her window. She won't. I try to explain my mistake in sign language—pointing to my eyes, telling her loudly that I've mistaken her car for that of a friend. I begin backing away from her into the street like an ungainly kid on roller skates.

My embarrassments are legion. I know the white cane has become a necessity for the maintenance of my psychological health. I enter bathrooms marked "Ladies," and entering restaurants, I trip down short flights of steps. I appear misty eyed and drunk and walk about in circles looking for exits and entrances.

Without the cane, who will understand me? But it will be another eighteen years before I receive proper Orientation and Mobility training. Before I will accept it.

■ ■ ■

IN ONE OF my last trips without a cane I visit the great Prado museum in Madrid, where I find I cannot see the famous paintings of Velázquez and Goya because they are hanging behind ropes that prohibit the vandals from drawing too close. Since I can't draw near, I see oceans of mud in vast gilded frames instead of the ceremonial world of court or the sprawl of lusty peasants.

I've waited years to get to the Prado, and now I'm wandering through its broad hallways thwarted by guards and ropes. Of course I should be carrying a white cane. But of course I'm carrying nothing except my sense of not-quite-belonging, which I'm fighting like a man swatting hornets.

At a souvenir counter I buy a museum guide—I'll read about the paintings I can't see—but the print is microscopic. Instead of a book, I find I'm holding a little cup full of sand.

The light in the Prado is alternately prismatic, then dark as a jail. I stand in the sunbeams under the oval skylights and watch the world break up into rainbows, then turn a corner into a great vaulted darkness, where an important painting hangs behind a veil, black as an abandoned lighthouse.

But I've traveled so far to see the paintings, and I hate to be circumscribed by tricks of the light, so I fall in with a group of

American tourists. They are dutifully following a Spanish woman tour-guide who is describing paintings in the gallery at which I've arrived. But she spots me as an impostor, a freeloading listener, and as I strain to see the fetlock of a painted horse, she points me out to the group.

"This man is not in our tour," she says. "Sir, you will have to leave."

And I walk from the museum, a flapping windmill of a man, and find myself doing a muddy umbrella-dance in the icy wet park. Two students approach and ask if I'll buy a comic book to help disabled schoolchildren. I give them some money and think that some kid will get a break.

■ ■ ■

DUSK IS THE hour when I'm most likely to misjudge the speed and flow of traffic. It's rush hour—people hurrying home in the autumn rush hour, some on foot, some in cars. In such moments I often feel prematurely aged: I want some help in crossing the street. I want to reach for someone's arm.

Ironically, though, as things visual are in doubt, they grow in unconventional beauty. Dear Jackson Pollock, I've entered your *Autumn Rhythm.* The irregular or sometimes certain flight of color and shape is a wild skein, a tassel of sudden blue here, a wash of red. The very air has turned to hand-blown glass with its imperfect bubbles of amethyst or hazel blue. I stand on the ordinary street corner as if I've awakened at the bottom of a stemware vase. The glassblower's molten rose has landed in my eyes.

I shift my glasses—a slow moon rises on my path, things appear and disappear, and the days are like Zen-autumn.

■ ■ ■

A BENEVOLENT SHAKESPEARE professor finds me a reader. Enter Ramona, a classics major who comes in the afternoons three days a week.

We sit in a sunbeam in a steep room somewhere toward the rear of the library. It's a storage space, old encyclopedias line the shelves. The librarian thinks no one will hear Ramona reading to me in this spot. He's given us two wooden chairs. We stack our books on them and sit on the floor. Soon we have a blanket, which we assiduously roll up and store each night in a closet.

Ramona is a tremendous reader, the shadowy forms of things, ideas, gestalt, whatever, they move as she talks. Together we cross the ancient hot plateaus where words are as mighty as numbers. She reads Gilgamesh, the poems of the Cid. And flat on my back in that tall room, I never fall asleep. What stranger miracles are there? Sometimes she stops, and I learn not to interrupt her silence: she's performing a calculation. It's a lesson for me in absorption. My own nervousness tends to exclude such moments.

Oddly enough, eros, syllables, and alchemy are facts, particularly in the lives of young people. Beside Ramona, listening, my habitual shyness around women begins to fall away. Outside the library, I find myself conversing with my female classmates with ease. For the first time, I discover how conversations between men and women can be like warm soap dissolving in a bath.

In the old student pub—a dark cellar, I meet a strange new girl named Bettina. We talk and drink German beer. Bettina is a polymath, angry, rebelling against her father, who is an executive at a television network.

"The bastard, he'd have been comfortable during the Crusades!" she says, and stubs her cigarette out in an ashtray on the bar.

With this altogether irreverent young woman, I experience puppy love. She's an Irish country girl with long, thrilling, unkempt red hair. Red leaning back toward gold.

Bettina cooks spaghetti over a gas ring in a basement. (She never has an apartment of her own, instead she occupies other people's places without self-consciousness. She knows everyone.) I accept a glass of wine, I'm wrapped in earth tones and sparks. My hands stink of Gauloises cigarettes, my fingers spasm from the nicotine.

She squeezes the juice of a lemon into the salad. Puts Tabasco in the pasta sauce. She throws raw carrot chunks in there too.

"Why are you putting carrots in the tomato sauce? That's disgusting!"

"Oh, shut up, if you'd eaten more carrots, your eyes would be better."

"I ate lots of carrots! My eyes went bad from masturbation!"

"Well, maybe you don't need to do that anymore."

I can't speak, because she's kissing me. It's a potent kiss, her tongue is wet and vital in my mouth.

She draws me to the floor, pulls down my pants, guides me inside her. I can't believe how quickly she does it, my brain is still stuck on the word *carrot*.

She's on top, loosening buttons down the front of her black dress. As her breasts touch my outstretched hands, I come with every ounce of my viscera. I come the way all virgin-boys should—with surrender and reverence. I'm trying to say something.

"It's okay," she whispers. "I'm wearing a diaphragm."

I start to rise on my elbows.

"I'm sorry, I—"

"Shhhhh!"

Her face closes in, her red hair falls over my eyes, tickles, smells faintly of shampoo. She guides my fingers gently to her clitoris. She's an open meadow! A birch tree at midsummer, the sunlight seeming to be above and inside her.

Like all virgins, I'm a narcissist: surely no one has ever experienced this abundant wet circle of girl before? Not like this!

I'm on a rug in a spot of lamplight. The sauce simmers behind us. There's a clatter of water pipes, there are apartments above. Dishes rattle somewhere. Bettina is astride me, and leaning, she kisses me forcefully, filling my mouth with her sip of cabernet.

For the first time the vast silence that follows sex expands in my chest.

"I love you!" I say it. "I love you!"

I begin to cry. I who cannot see a woman's face, who can't look someone in the eye, I, I, who, what, never thought this could happen. I'm crying in earnest, copious sparkles.

"Shhhhh!"

She arches her back, I slip from her, a little fish, laughing and weeping.

Bettina refastens her dress, retrieves a tortoiseshell hair clasp, arranges it, sings very softly some lines from Yeats: " 'Ah penny, brown penny, I am looped in the loops of her hair.' "

■ ■ ■

NIGHTS. NOVEMBER. BOOKS. Smoke. Pierre Reverdy. Emily Dickinson. The windows open, a sweet smell of fallen leaves. I stroke Bettina's neck as she reads from Rexroth's Chinese poems: " 'The same clear glory extends for ten thousand miles. The twilit trees are full of crows.' "

I'm unimaginably blessed. The crystallography of sharpened syntax, image, her voice behind it, wash of water on stones.

" 'My soul wandered, happy, sad, unending.' " (Neruda)

" 'The branches are dying of love.' " (Lorca)

" 'Show me, dear Christ, thy spouse, so bright and clear.' " (Donne)

" 'Here is the shadow of truth, for only the shadow is true.' " (Warren)

. . .

IN THE LIBRARY Bettina finds a box of discarded records. These are Caedmon recordings of Yeats, an actor reading Baudelaire, poems by Carl Sandburg, John Crowe Ransom. The recordings are in miserable condition. And there at the bottom of the pile is a recorded bird-watching disk. A British narrator talks the listener through encounters with dozens of different birds. The birds sing on command, precise, silver, optimistic.

"Listen to the plover!" says the voice. "He's stirring on a spring morning!"

The plover obeys, lets loose its porous notes.

"Now the nightingale. Bird of poetry!"

The nightingale sounds brighter and better rested than the plover. Clearly it is a happy bird.

"The blackbird."

"The oriole."

In some places the needle sticks. The oriole hiccups over and over.

Here come the wild swans.

I'm completely jazzed: all my life I've been a stranger in this neighborhood. I've never seen a bird. Now, hearing them has made a place in my imagination. The birds! The damned birds! I've been missing out on something huge. But where are they?

Someone tells me about the ornithology collection in the biology building. I go there alone on a Saturday, when I know that the building will be deserted. The birds are arranged in display cases on both sides of the first-floor corridor. I press my nose to the glass specimen case and try not to breathe, for breathing fogs the glass. I see cocoon shapes, brown as cordovan shoes. These are the taxidermied and long-fallen members of the parliament, as strange to me as Roman coins and nails.

The labs are empty, the lights off. There is a hum of large refrigerators, a percolating sound. I tap the glass case with my forefinger, and it swings open as if by magic! Perhaps some student assistant has forgotten to lock the case!

Imagine never having seen a bird. And now your hands are free to explore the vagaries of the bird-tomb. How weightless they are, light as dinner rolls! But the feathers are stiff, almost lacquered, like the tiny ribs of a corset I once held in an antique shop. This can't be what a live bird's plumage would feel like. These birds are stiff, Victorian, spent.

But what a miracle of pipe stems and ligatures, the legs and wings joined with such supple delicacy.

I lift a large thing from its perch, hold it to my face, just barely making out its predatory look. A hawk? It's large as a basketball, light as a throwaway newspaper.

Here I am, twentysomething, standing in a deserted corridor, fondling birds. I feel like a frotteurist: a person who has orgasms from casual touch with strangers. I'm some kind of pervert, alone with these dead birds, running my hands over their heads, tracing their beaks with my fingernails. What if a security guard were to appear and ask me what I'm doing?

"I'm blind, sir, and this is my first experience with birds!"

"My name is Kid Geronimo, and I live in the elevator!"

"Have you ever touched a plover, sir?"

"My name is Wigglesworth, I'm searching for insects."

This is a lifelong habit, imaginary conversations with authority figures, usually when I'm touching something, when I'm on the verge of an understanding.

All the birds smell like vintage hats. As I run my hands over their prickly backs, I put names to them, since I have no idea what they are.

"Leather-breasted barnacle chomper."

"Blue-throated Javanese son of Zero."

Outside I sit under a tree and listen to the living catbirds, a thrush, the chickadee. What I wish for is to see a live bird. So one afternoon shortly thereafter, I convince my friend and teacher Jim Crenner to go bird-watching with me. Jim is a poet, a student of anything that possesses color. He is a mosaic man with a Peterson's guide and at least two pairs of binoculars.

We walk into a meadow, talking of poets, Leopardi, Rumi, Eliot.

Jim knows I can't see well but figures he can point me to colors, fix me on a glittering stone from Ravenna, a goldfinch on a fencepost.

"Hold still, right there is a fat finch big as a Spanish gold piece!" he says, whispering through his mustache, as if he were reading aloud in one of his classes.

"There's a red-winged blackbird."

"A vireo."

"A scarlet tanager."

How toothsome they all sound! How thrilling it must be to spy them on their April branches, blond chaff from the skies, afterthoughts of a blue atmosphere.

When I look through binoculars, I see a coral blue/green bubble, perhaps my own eye, but nothing like a bird. I can't quite bring myself to tell this to Jim, who is in a rapture of color and evolutionary wonder.

"To think these things evolved from primal mud without a god!" he says, alert to the sheer improbability of our planet. But by now I realize I am looking at the blue dish of self. My field glasses are trained on my own optic nerves.

I have a major bird thirst, something untranslatable, I can't share it, can't cry aloud at my frustration. Instead I pretend.

"Can you see him? He's right on that post, fat and horny," says Jim, and I look into my own dish of thickened green and say, "Look at him jump!" At the moment I say it, I mean it. I can see that bird hopping up and down, that goldfinch jumping like a penny on a railroad track.

I agree with everything Jim sees, adding my own intensifiers and adjectives. I don't want to tell him I can't see the damned things, fearing it will make him self-conscious, for then our outing will become an exercise in description. He'll have to tell me what they look like. And I will have to appreciate them all the more. By pretending to see, I'm sparing us an ordeal. Sure I'm faking it with the binoculars, gloating over imaginary bluejays, but I'm alone with my own imagination, listening casually to an enthusiastic friend, my blindness locked away for the time.

I think Jim imagines I've seen some birds, and maybe I have.

7

ON A SPRING night in my junior year, I sit up late drinking Tennessee whiskey under an oak tree with my friend T.J. He's leaving for Paris and Rome for the summer. He talks softly about the trains, people spreading out unimaginable picnics in the railway cars, great wine, the flashing greenery of southern France outside.

"The nights smell like wild violets. You get off the train in some little town, and the whole place smells like tiny fucking flowers!"

"You, my friend, are full of horseshit! Those French towns don't smell any different than the towns in Nebraska. You get a different kind of hay fever there, that's all."

"No K-boy, the violets are so thick, the wild boars munch on 'em and get drunk and wander right into town. I think you need to go there sometime, go to Provence, eat the food."

"Yeah, but I agree with Williams, the New Jersey poet. All his friends were in Paris, Ford Madox Ford, Ezra Pound, Gertrude Stein. He said he could see it all right there in Paterson."

"He's the one who wrote that poem about seeing the broken glass along the roadside on the way to the hospital?"

"Yeah."

"Well, I'd rather see the Pyrenees. The clouds sail right up to these mountains and break like Mexican piñatas, the rain spills out in gold—it's incredible. And the Basque people are living the way people lived hundreds of years ago, herding sheep, making music. It's just fucking great. Screw Paterson! What've they got? A boarded-up Woolworth and a river full of stolen shopping carts."

He's really working the whiskey, taking good pulls. And so am I.

"You oughta go somewhere. Go with Bettina, she's going to Athens. Go to the Greek islands, have some fucking grape leaves."

It's true, Bettina is going to Athens. Forty students and two professors will live in a hotel in the Plaka. They'll read Thucydides and Homer, tour the temples of Poseidon with bottles of ouzo in their backpacks.

I can't tell him how afraid the idea of traveling makes me. I know the campus. I know the sidewalks. Everything else is the great jungle of night, the unfamiliar has vines and teeth. My blind-passing-for-sighted universe is very small, as small as a simple town square.

Later that night I lie back in bed feeling as if I'm coated with coal dust. It's the spring semester, honeysuckle wafts in through the window.

How can I go anywhere? How in the hell can I go to Athens when I can't even read a fucking book?

And of course I don't have any words for my quandary. I recite other people's words. Lines from the poets:

"It so happens I am tired of being a man." (Pablo Neruda)

"How strange to think of giving up all ambition." (Robert Bly)

"Black milk of daybreak we drink it at nightfall." (Paul Celan)

All words, loose, no focus available. Memory retrieving syllables. No lenses thick enough to bring me Bettina's face. I'm in awe of her fingertips, her tongue. I murmur over and over, "I love you," drowning in anxious seconds of proximity, a blind kid afraid this first-time closeness will vanish as soon as she knows how helpless I am in the unfamiliar streets of anyplace. Any place. Any.

Even while I know she knows I can't see, I still need to appear sighted. Manage my steps. Look forceful. Race-walk in the white foam.

I'm on fire from the whiskey. The bed is damp with my sweat. There's a mourning dove outside. In my tiny kitchen the early light falls on the bread and dishes, a shine that stabs my watering eyes. I can barely find the faucet. How will I go anywhere?

■　■　■

"THEY STILL HAVE some space in the program," Bettina says, somewhat indistinctly. She's taken to hand-rolling her cigarettes—she's licking the glue.

She lights it, a bulging finger's width of crumbling tobacco.

"You should come! We'll climb hills in Crete, sleep under the sapphire stars. We'll eat feta. Put drachmas in our penny loafers."

"Bettina, will you read to me?"

"Of course I'll read to you. I'll mispronounce the name of every hero in the *Iliad*!"

But reading is just the tip of the iceberg. I need help getting places, avoiding cars. How will I find the hotel? Manage in the ruins?

She hands me a clownish cigarette, a paper guppy.

"We can look for Byron's graffiti."

I imagine Byron with a fez on his head, wielding a Magic Marker.

And so it happens I'm on a plane bound for the Mediterranean world. I'm in terror. "Now we see as through a glass darkly," says Augustine, referring to mortal seeing, our failure to know the true world as God must see it.

I'm looking through the dark glass.

Aboard the 737 I ask for a martini.

■ ■ ■

THE PLAKA IS sulfuric, blue with smoke from motor scooters, buses, cars. There is oil on the paving stones. I'm beneath a wave of light, my arms and legs so tense, I must look like a child wearing clean clothes.

Hypersensitive, holding my breath, I try to navigate the narrow walks impossible for footing. People are bumping me from all directions. I release my breath without rhythm, don't know where I should point my face.

Bettina has disappeared, as usual. I find myself in the company of Del and Shepard, two affable college boys who have studied the map. Del is tall and extremely thin. He laughs at everything. Shepard is from Berkeley, California, he has long straw hair tied in a ponytail. He carries a woven shoulder bag from Guatemala.

He has notebooks, cigarettes, a Swiss army knife for opening wine or slicing cheeses.

We walk through an open air market. I'm struck in the shoulder by something pointed. An umbrella? It's not raining.

I'm pallid, nervous as a horse in blinders, working my nostrils. Now Del is shoving something in my hand.

"Hey, check out the prick on this!"

I'm holding a figurine of Bacchus sporting a huge erection.

A vendor is shouting at me to put it back, or maybe he wants me to buy it. I thrust it toward the talking shadows. Keep moving.

Del is laughing.

"Whatsa matter, you don't like art?"

"When you find Aphrodite, lemme know!" Shepard sings aloud Pete Seeger's "Old Time Religion"—something, something, " 'Aphrodite, Aphrodite, she wears a see-through nightie!' "

Shepard knows his folk music, plays fluent guitar.

"Let's have a smoke," he says. "There's a bar, we can get a drink."

Inside it smells of wet masonry. There's a click of ceiling fans. No voices or music.

There's a tangled translucence in front of me, a warm hand is suddenly on my arm.

"Hi! You buy me drink?"

She lightly strokes my cheek. "Come with me!"

Other voices are in the gloom.

"Hi! You like music?"

"My name is Miriam!"

Giggling.

We're at a table, I hit it with my knee. The girl with her hand on mine now spins me deftly into a chair.

"How about you buy me a drink?"

"Me too," says Miriam.

Although I can't see, I suspect that Miriam is sitting on Del's lap.

"Me too," says a third, leaning on Shepard. "You buy me a rum and Coke?"

Shepard laughs. "Sorry, I'm on a scholarship!" Del laughs with evident good humor. "Me too. I'm on financial aid!"

In the grimy half-dark we've become six monkeys. My glasses are passed around like a pocket watch swiped from a tourist in the primate house.

A waiter appears with drinks, but Del and Shepard are rising to leave.

"No drinks," says Del. "We haven't ordered any drinks!"

"Yes. You pay. Two hundred drachma!" The bartender seems to be in our way. And he is joined now by five or six silent men. "Easy," he says. "You pay."

The scene washes through me, I'm still sitting. One of the girls runs her fingers along the hair of my arm.

"Nice," she says.

"It's fake," I say, "Sears, Roebuck." Shepard snorts.

"Give me my glasses." I stretch my hand out. I don't know who actually holds them.

For some reason I feel an exotic dignity, and I stand up.

"Give me the *fucking glasses!*"

Somebody puts them in my hand.

My eyes ache in that way that focuses the brain, as toothaches sometimes will.

"I have syphilis. Bad eyes," I say to one of the girls, and point to my face. It's a moment of pure telegraphy. We leave without opposition.

The glasses, when I put them on, give up a strange perfume.

■ ■ ■

ATHENS IS A brilliant treasury. All its displays are too expensive, and so I don't actually view them. I'm like the woman who sits outside the Byzantine church wrapped in her blanket. Bettina and I pass her each morning as we walk toward Constitution Square for coffee. We give her money, and she croaks a blessing.

I discover silence in all the abundances. I listen. In the national museum I follow the tour-guide's descriptions of the great statue of Zeus. For me he's a green-going-to-turquoise dragon, a galleon, a huge blue industrial vat. Someone tells me he looks astonished at his power. The ordinary rooms of the museum are my private topiary gardens, hedgerows shaped like dancing bears or griffins rise around me. Here's a tip of orange flame. A burning bush from the Old Testament. These are the things I see. Others examine Cycladic pottery, but there in front of me a scratched soul rises straight from the navel of the earth in a gray spume. How did they ever get it inside a glass case?

Bettina tells me that Achilles had a tiny head.

"The helmets are shaped like pears, and they're no bigger than a Coke can!"

"What if Achilles had a big head, did they hammer the thing on? Was it a one-size-fits-all culture?"

"Judging by the helmets, it was!"

"There's no mention in the *Iliad* of the mighty Greeks standing still while they pound the helmets on their heads."

We're sitting on a portico outside the museum, the sunlight is quite bright by noon.

"It's a heroic culture, whether it's celebrating or mourning. There are no ordinary people." I'm starting to fulminate as tourists pass in all directions.

"I mean, you know, they killed the disabled unless they were very old and distinguished like Homer."

"Goddesses/whores; heroes/slaves—oh, *shit*!" Bettina is scratching at her head. "That fucking bird just shit on my head!"

"Hold on! I'll catch it, and we'll read its entrails!"

"Fuck! You can read its entrails on my head!"

I rummage around my backpack, produce a set of index cards. "We can scrape it off with these."

"No wonder they wore those helmets."

• • •

BLIND NIGHTS. RAIN falling hard. Strange neighborhoods. Bettina. Tastes of sour wine. Taxicabs. Mystery of footsteps. Hold her hand. My mobility is passion. Now we're running, rain turning into hail. The electric lights have gone out.

We enter the black lobby of a strange hotel. There's no one at the desk. The storm is now furious. Somewhere windows are breaking. Bettina has my hand, is leading me up a curving stairwell.

We lie down on an empty bed in the middle of a storm. We've found the last hotel in the world.

• • •

BY DAY I walk in the blazing ruins, the light so fierce, I must continually find places to sit where I can cover my eyes.

One can be seasick from vision impairments. You're looking through a crack in a door. That's your right eye. The other eye is molten glass: the midday world is a searchlight. Horrible. Sweat springs to the back of your neck.

I've made the mistake of buying sandals, and now I have two broken toes, which are blue in the light of scrutiny.

Somewhere before me the professor is talking. The open-air lecture concerns the influence of landscape on the design of Greek temples. I picture slaves felling the forests, the trunks of Greek pine assembled as rollers, the immense marble hauled with armies of men and horses.

I wonder if blind slaves dragged the marble up the hills. Did they have blind slaves? I know the Romans had blind prostitutes. Did the Greeks have blind prostitutes?

Outside my hotel the blind lottery sellers sing all morning. They walk about with their white sticks and hundreds of colored tickets hanging from their clothes. I've bumped into them when I've tried to walk alone.

As the professor talks, I find my way behind a column and let myself vomit. I'm a stumbling, sunlit desecration. Crickets sing among the stones.

On my knees in all this light, I suspect the day will last forever. Thank God there's a softer wind. A froth of seeds like milkweed rises before me. The nystagmus is stabbing me from my pupils on down into my guts. I bow my head before the Parthenon. Every stone appears to move. To the tourists it must seem as though I'm in a state of reverence.

"You don't look so well," Shepard says, scrutinizing my odd detachment.

"I'm going to be sick, I think it's a migraine."

Shepard walks me down from the Parthenon and finds me a cab. Back at the hotel I cling to the cold walls of the water closet. My eyes have a bloody pulse, they seem about to burst.

And so I lie down on the cold floor. I want to sleep for a while, then open my eyes on the first light of morning.

That's all.

Let the Athenian afternoon continue its business.

I promise myself that I won't suffocate. Not in the Hotel Hermes.

There's a poem unwinding inside my head. Yeats.

"Upon the brimming water . . . nine-and-fifty swans . . ."

I try to hold still and float.

And I do fall asleep on that bathroom floor.

■ ■ ■

MY SELF-LOATHING wrestles with the amethyst water of being alive and awake. I'm on the deck of a boat sailing to Delos. Bettina has brought me honey and yogurt.

We arrive at the harbor at dusk, when each headlight looms as large as the harvest moon. Solid shapes divide like windblown strands of web. The faces leaning toward me trail gauzy light, petals on a wet black bough. In such moments I want to reach for someone's arm. Dear Proteus, master of shapes, let me touch your sleeve.

I want to tell her, this girl who reads to me, how each shape and color is a restraint, that the issue isn't merely the pages of books. But I don't have words, so fragile are the roots of masculinity, its first leaves.

From the hillside above the town lies the dark shell of the harbor's basin, pinpoints of lights. We've spread out sleeping bags, unwrapped a loaf of bread. We have wine, cheese, olives.

We lie back.

■ ■ ■

I'VE BARELY AWAKENED the next morning, and I'm reeling like a victim. It's my own hand at my throat. I'm chewing my morning bread, and covetousness is swallowing.

I'm the pint-sized king of envy.

My words are tinctured with it. I envy all who see things. The goddamned bird-watchers, motorcycle riders, butterfly collectors, I envy them all. I envy the blissful lamb, I envy and envy and envy.

I'm lucky. Down deep I know it. I have colors. And although the visual eludes me, I have some of its shapes as keepsakes. In and out of the haze I go, feeling with my toes. O Lord, let me look urgent, let me move with agility.

Bettina awakens.

It should be simple.

Begin with the lips. MMMMMMMMMMMM.

"I'm blind."

Now the guh, guh sound, please.

G G G G G

"Give me your elbow, please. Guide me through the stones."

There's fire in the sea, the hills smell of sage.

I imagine the words come forth. That I can say them. Then Bettina will offer me her arm with understanding, steer me with infinite concern and caring. I'm free to turn my face to the morning. Free to imagine the generous piece of being blind. To take Bettina's arm and, together in spirit, go down to the harbor in search of morning coffee.

How simple this should be.

Sunstreaks fall across the sails. I imagine I hear her say, "Those are sails like you might imagine the Phoenicians had." Now I know what she's seeing, linked with her eyes and her splendid ideas.

We climb to the ruined temple. She steers me, says, "Low branch"; says, "Step up"; I move knee-deep in shoals of milk, but I have no fear.

"These are the lions of Delos," she says. "They appear to be leaping into the sky."

Imagine. I don't have to play the bird-watching game.

But I do.

I make a poor choice and keep my mouth shut.

As a result, I dance in a thistle dance, something atavistic, older than the stone lions. Among spiky flowers I'm headless, lifting my feet, moving in bloodless melancholy.

Bettina sits against a stone and pulls out a drawing tablet. As she sketches, I smoke and move my hands back and forth in the dirt.

8

—

MY OVERSTUFFED LEATHER briefcase is filled with uncompleted assignments: a term paper on Thucydides, for example, something about Pericles and his funeral oration to the Athenians. There's a journal I should have kept about the reading I did not do while I stumbled through the ancient streets of the Peloponnese.

Back on campus, ashamed of this self-perceived failure, I brood and unconsciously take up a childhood habit of relentlessly pulling hair from my body. I strip my sideburns and then raid my mustache, leaving bent hairs all across the unread pages. I must go to a barber and have the rest of my hair professionally removed. I have to find a way to finish these books, but already my final semester has started. I'm exhausted, giddy, sleepless; sometimes I have to drink myself to sleep. Then nights are dreamtime:

Often, I'm swimming around in a lake where strangers also swim. Everyone swims with their clothes on, their pockets ballooning with air. A pagoda floats before me. A dignitary waves and smiles. He has gold teeth.

My hands and arms are white as the bellies of fish. I raise them out of the brine.

A boat must have sunk, there are floating deck chairs. But the whole thing is weirdly calm. A huge birdcage floats up with an enormous parrot inside. The water and the sky are iron gray. A basket of flowers floats past. Now a swimming dog. I put my face under water, begin a long dive.

A boat lies on its side, the hull open in places, all the rooms are still illuminated. I swim into a drawing room with gold curtains and heavy brocaded Turkish furniture—the walls are of paneled wood. There are decorative trees waving in alcoves.

Am I supposed to be finding something? I think so.

Here's a shoe that slips from my hands.

And now I'm in the street, swimming on my belly. No, it's a corridor. The doors of staterooms are open, ruby light inside each room. Scarves floating and women's underthings.

A telephone.

An icebox.

Shelf of books. Fish swimming there.

Have you ever touched a live fish? Nothing stays in my fingers.

T.J. reads to me from John Donne. His Carolina softness of speech coupled with Donne's metrical worship of God's grace is a lovely thing.

" 'Stand still, and I will read to thee / A lecture, love, in love's philosophy.'

" 'I am two fools. I know, / For loving, and for saying so. . . .'

"Man," says T.J., "man oh man, he's sweet as a peach!"

"Keep reading!" I tell him.

"I'm never going to get out of this college alive."

He reads, and the words waver. Regret. Forgetting. Absences. The immensities of time. The Christian blame, love, sex, healings.

He reads, raising music from a yellowed page.

" 'Teach me to hear mermaids singing.' "

The night is falling fast. The poplars stand like black masts in the new cold.

" 'So my devout fits come and go away / Like a fantastic ague: save that here / Those are my best days as I shake with fear.' "

We walk across the campus, our respective hearts beating with those immensities of action and choice that growing up must entail. Only contingencies can be played with. The two of us believe this.

We've recently lost our respective girlfriends. In 1977 the young women are as thrilled as the boys to have their fields of choice—but the boyhearts can't quite comprehend this. We're bruised, like those apples Robert Frost will save for cider. Goodbye, Bettina. Basking in the novelty of a girl's attention, I thought she was the one I would marry. There will be others, but I don't know this, and in any event, poetry is the most reliable lover.

Alone in my college room, I sit with the lights off for a while. It's my burden of irony to love poetry. I want to understand burdens, reckon them like a box of foreign coins remaining from a trip. If reading is evanescent, then it's doubly good? Physical reading eludes me, and being read to is inefficient, even hopeless. Being able to make out print for short bursts of time is not reading, it's deciphering, by definition a "nonliterary" experience. And while blindness keeps one at a remove from the world, words, our common stock, are real as the knuckles in soup.

Who needs to read fast? In Nepal, when someone dies, their relatives string garlands of yellow flowers and float them across the sacred river, a bridge to the beyond. This is not assembly-line work.

So I read slowly.

■ ■ ■

HEADING TOWARD THE collegiate finish line, I'm seasick, and all too often hung over. In my anxiety, I've taken up hard liquor and drink Jim Beam almost nightly. Sometimes I wake up to find I've broken a chair or, worse, have made an ass of myself by falling into a fireplace at a party or vomiting wildly on someone's Persian rug.

Pregraduation pressure is standard. Students at the ends of college careers are known to come unglued like old banjos, their strings popping. It's late May, the season of motorcycle accidents and failed courses. Luckily my doggedness pays off, and though I can't explain how I did it, I graduate from college with highest honors in English and a cum laude diploma. Still, my last months are just plain vertigo.

I learn to swallow aspirin without water.

Sometimes, between classes, in the middle of the day, I sit in the chapel, my hollow tree. Tears run down my cheeks. My hair, long again now, falls into the tears. In the darkest corner of the chapel I chew at the ends of my mustache. To others, it must look as if I've lost a loved one.

Sitting in the pew, there are no disciples or messiahs, just the tears and, occasionally, the cartoon imagination:

"Hello. My name is Evelyn Wood, the queen of speed reading courses, I used to be like you, a wretch who wanted to read Proust!"

She's wearing a silver turban with an amethyst at the center.

"One day I was standing by the mimeograph machine, and I said to myself, Evelyn, you can become a speed reader! And you know, I did?!"

"Yeah, Evelyn, there's only one problem. I'm a blind wretch. B.W.! Milton without daughters."

"Oh. That is a problem. I'm so sorry, dearie!"

Poof!

Even so, without gurus, there are moments outside the classroom. Five miles from campus, on a long walk through orchards and freshly turned meadows, I find an enormous oak tree that has the rusted blade of a scythe implanted in its trunk. Farmers leaving for the Civil War stuck those blades in the trees as they went off to battle, their version of tying a ribbon around a fencepost. To this day scythe-trees remain standing, their soldiers having never come home. The oak tree that I find is more remarkable still, because high in the branches a red-tailed hawk has made her nest. She doesn't like me to sit under her tree, but I do, just to hear her hawksong as she circles above my head.

■ ■ ■

ONE HOT AFTERNOON when my dread at not knowing where to go has reached a fever pitch, I fall in with Shepard, who's on his way to the post office. I've applied to graduate schools and am anticipating some news.

As of this moment, I don't know what I'm doing. The world's oblivious martial music doesn't have a part for me. I'm like Woody Allen in *Take the Money and Run*—he plays the cello in a marching band, drags the huge instrument and his stool in a hilarious effort to keep pace with the parade.

Since there are no practical methods of employment for someone who can't see, where can I possibly go? In my fatigue, chiseling at noon air, pupils alchemized, hot liquids becoming wax, who will give me something to do?

"I just had a daydream. Evelyn Wood, the speed reading maven, was wearing a silver turban and talking about Proust."

"You need coffee. You have what they used to call 'the vapors.'"

Shepard is jaunty. After graduation he's going to Boulder, Colorado, where he plans to do carpentry, make musical instruments. Perform in bars.

I think of Leadbelly, the "king of the 12-string," the blues singer from Louisiana. He used to tour throughout the South in the twenties with sidekick Blind Lemon Jefferson. They rode the trains as fugitives, stowaways, played the blues.

Maybe I can be Blind Lemon, follow Shepard to Boulder. But then there's the dependence thing. Who could live like Blind Lemon and follow someone around, wait on strange streets for Leadbelly to return with a sausage and a jar of whiskey? No. I can't follow Leadbelly, live in suspense the way I did one day in a Greek city: Is Bettina coming back? She said she would. What if she doesn't? How awful is that?

Roaming in needy tandem with the others who can see is no substitute for a room of one's own—this I understand. I need to live somehow, I don't know, like Carl Jung, who had a stone turret for his personal ruminations. Robinson Jeffers, he had Tor

House, a homemade castle by the sea in Carmel, California. Montaigne had a tower of some kind. Shit, I don't need a tower. A tent will do. Didn't young Robert Lowell pitch a tent on Alan Tate's lawn? But he could read. I need a companion. But goddammit! I hate companions! They talk and laugh, and then they complain or they want something. Nothing's worse than other people's wants!

At the post office Shepard hangs out front, smoking and razzing some cronies. I go inside and retrieve my letters. I need to find someone to read them. Shepard's having too much fun, and these letters are too momentous. I stand pressing them to my forehead while people hurry around me.

On television Johnny Carson puts a crimson towel on his head and plays "The Great Karnak"—a disreputable psychic who holds sealed envelopes to his forehead and gives the salty answer to the unseen riddle. It's a great gag: no one looks less psychic than Carson, who appears to be like the average suburbanite. And that the greatest powers of discernment would be wasted on piffle, this is funny!

Who will tell me what the letters say?

I walk to the swimming pool. I swim several times a week. It's the only way to keep my aching back and shoulders in some semblance of flexibility. And over time I've been befriended by an elderly Syrian man, Solomon, who dispenses towels and levity.

"So here they are, Sol, read 'em and weep."

"What? Five armies have drafted you?"

"Yeah, the blind infantry is competitive!"

"Well let's see, this one's from the University of Iowa."

"Read me that one."

Iowa has a graduate school renowned for its poets. Since I discovered poetry, I've dreamed of going there.

"Hold on, hold on, here it is. 'I'm pleased to inform you that you have been admitted for graduate study at the Writers' Workshop.' Hey, you're a Hawkeye!"

9

—

IN IOWA CITY I wonder how to find readers to guide me through my private arcanum of Egyptian lore, Finnish folk tales, recondite babblings of Ezra Pound, concordances, small literary journals, mimeographed poems.

Because I am blind, I qualify for social security assistance. I've been pushed to apply by my father, who, though generally unable to converse about blindness, has read in the newspaper that financial support is available for the visually impaired. Though I greet his unsolicited advice with near-total silence, I find when I'm on my own that the stipend is too significant to ignore.

In the federal building I fill out forms with the help of a very pink man who has an enormous smile and the kind of affability that you never find in the east. It's true, what they say about the heartland. The people out here are genial and optimistic, even interested.

"Say, have you met Barry from the Iowa Commission yet?" he asks since we're on the subject of disability support.

I don't know what the Iowa Commission is. To me, it sounds vaguely ominous, like a group that might have investigated Alger Hiss. But he's talking about the Commission for the Blind, an organization funded by the state.

A week later I'm visited by Barry, my first ever blind adviser. He's very secure, compact, cool, and, yes, he's affable too. He wears a wide-brimmed Italian hat and a leather jacket. He carries a folding white cane. Sometimes he uses it to find the curbs or stairs, at other moments he breaks it down neatly, like a hinged yardstick, and puts it into the back pocket of his jeans. I've never seen anyone like him. He's the second angel in my life after Mrs. Edinger, who thought I could read with a little extra effort.

Barry stands in my doorway and laughs.

"So you want to embrace disability?" he says. (On the telephone I'd said some such thing.) "Me too! The trouble is," he adds, "disability is so hard to find!"

"That's a blind joke. You can't fool me. That's one of those blind jokes!"

Barry's in my apartment now, opening a big salesman's case.

"Let's see. You have the retinopathy of prematurity?"

"Yeah."

"Went to public school?"

"Yup."

"I bet that was no picnic!"

"It's still no picnic!"

He's putting something together, it sounds like a camera tripod.

"Ever use one of these? It's a pocket tape recorder with a foot pedal. You put the pedal under the desk and turn it on or off when you want to record. It leaves your hands free to hold other things, which hopefully are going to be exclusively in magnified print."

"Books aren't widely available in large print, are they?"

"No, but we're going to get you what's called a CCTV. It's a closed circuit television with a high-resolution camera. The camera scans the page, and the TV makes the print very large. You can put anything under this thing. We will also have readers for you. And through the state library you can get your usual talking books on records and tapes . . .

"The point is, there's no one solution to blindness like yours. For brief moments you can see, although probably not well. Other times it's impossible, and likely painful. Am I right?"

My mouth is open, at least figuratively. Here's a stranger who understands me: this is as beautiful and unforeseeable as the guest who appears in poems by Kabir, the guest who is really a god, but a god who has known you all along.

Barry walks around the room, surveying with real acumen.

"Is this a bicycle?"

"Yeah, I—"

"Get rid of it!"

"Well, I—"

"Blind people have no business riding bicycles, even though lots of them try it. Show me your work area."

I point out my kitchen table. A jumble of papers, books, a rat's nest, in fact.

"Okay. I'm going to get you some organizers. You can't spend your time searching and searching for things."

He pauses. It's starting to rain outside, the windows are spattering.

"This is the day when all the leaves come down," he says. "I hate it because for a few days the sidewalks are just like soapy floors.

"Tell me," he says, after we've walked down the street for tea. "Your parents didn't know how to help you with this, right?"

"Well, I don't think they have the words for it. I mean they know some necessary vocabulary, *retinal detachment*, *legal blindness*, and the like, but the emotional language—they don't have that."

"So you didn't really talk about it?"

"Not really. I think they felt guilty."

"Well you know, that's not surprising, blindness is depressing. It's in many ways not the hardest disability, although pain comparisons are never really useful, but it's a medicine ball when you find out you're going blind, or that your kid is blind."

"Did your parents talk about it?"

"I didn't go blind until my early thirties—diabetes. My parents were pretty good, helped me read about it, find doctors. But there are lots of kids who have grieving parents, and often too little gets said."

As we walk back up Dubuque Street to my apartment, he says, "You need to carry one of these." He flourishes the cane. "You have to accept how you really are. The cane is about being alive. It serves all kinds of functions. Other people understand your situation. You spend a lot less time explaining yourself. Cars slow down—at least most of them! And you can bump into women with impunity. That's how I met my wife!"

I listen to Barry's views—in fact, I listen very hard. He's telling me that blindness isn't a game. He's gently excusing me my quiet exploration but giving me a proper nudge. And like all proper nudges, it's frightening. He's directing me into the open, the cane is an invitation to be nude in public. I'll have to take this under advisement, stew it for a while.

■ ■ ■

A WEEK LATER during a terrible heat wave, classes begin. The Writers' Workshop is in a modern building on the shore of the Iowa River. It's humid down here, steam rises from the water, and you can almost hear the willow trees breathing. Poets and fiction writers have gathered here for decades; the teachers reminisce, and the graduate students take long walks, fill their notebooks, discover imported black tea.

The classes are wildly various; some are like group therapy, while others become gatherings of cooperative scientists. In every session the poet apprentice reads aloud from his or her work while nine others read from copies. A noted poet-elder presides over the discussions that follow.

During the two years I spent there, the faculty used a mimeograph machine to reproduce student work. Every Wednesday stapled packets of purple typing were distributed for our editorial scrutiny. The object was to mark those pages thoroughly. In classes we would refer to those notes as we spoke.

The pages were impossible for me to read, and asking classmates to read them aloud and inscribe my critical responses proved awkward. Young poets bristle, spit, feel lofty defeats, sparkle like mica. Each poem hangs over them like a dirigible that must be shot at, run from, dispelled by incantation, or saluted.

Poetry writing is a monastic activity. And monks will tell you that devotion to God is both anger and love. That's why so many take vows of silence. But at Iowa we took vows that we would speak.

One week into the semester, I'm visited by Terence, a poet-classmate who has offered to read "the worksheets" to me. He's thin, sallow, his hands are always branching in the abstract air as he recites lines from the French poets: Mallarmé, Nerval. He's a smart young poet, though he doesn't like his classmates. This I find out as he reads. I remember it sounding something like this:

"Okay. Here's a poem by Miriam. Cough." (He says the word *cough*.) "Oh, it's another sea-goddess effusion. She has a trunk's worth of these!"

"Please, just read it, I need to formulate my own responses, okay?"

"All right, here we go. (Cough.) No title. 'The brave one sleeps for a time / Of course the past is with her, / Beauty dissolved into thingness, narrow streets / Where she goes disguised.' "

He pauses.

"Oh, *please*! The fucking sea is dying of love! I can't *stand* it!"

He lights a cigarette.

"Hey, do you have any Coca-Cola? I can't read this without Coca-Cola."

"Sorry, I don't have any Coke. Want some orange juice?"

"No. Orange juice is revolting."

"Instant coffee?"

"Never mind."

I hear him flicking ashes into something.

"Hey, you want an ashtray?"

"No, thanks."

Where is he putting his ashes?

"Keep reading, okay?"

"Right. 'Even Odysseus / In cold solitude / Can't see her now.' "

He stops again.

"It's just *Antony and Cleopatra* redux!"

"Terence, *everything* is *Antony and Cleopatra* redux. Let's keep going."

"Let's skip *her*. Here's one by Roger. I call him Harpo because he's a musical surrealist."

He starts in on Roger's poem.

"This is titled 'Night Dogs.' 'Here they are, their sponge brains full of blood / Sniffing behind the peasant auberge. / Incroyable! The kitchen girl gives them tripe, tongue and testicles / Day old bread . . .'"

Pause.

"Peasants *never* give away those things!"

He's really indignant!

"Roger is imitating a Czech poet, Miroslav Holub. Czechs throw their tripe away, not the French!"

He's now under a spell, an intestinal reading of national character.

After he goes, I find that he's put five cigarettes into my souvenir dish from the Holy Land, a wooden plate with a glass bubble at the center that holds water from the Jordan River.

Around the edges are pictures of John the Baptist, Jesus, the disciples. It's my little article of holy kitsch, given to me by my grandmother. Sometimes when my eyes are very tired, I put it to my ear like a sea shell and listen to the Jordan water. (Terence has burned its perimeter.) It's perfect!

■   ■   ■

IN THE CLASSROOM the criticism is heated, and since I can't read the worksheets, I sit in the fog. Sometimes I raise my hand and say things like, "Paul Klee made dolls for children, primitives, hand-painted. This poem has that quality of the reliquary, the universal unconscious."

What else can I do? I listen with care, but the fluorescent lights produce a vitreous squinting, and through each wordy argument, I'm again the boy in the first grade listening hard to make sense of something on the blackboard. When it comes time for me to read my own poem, I recite it from memory, holding the worksheet as though I might be reading aloud. In retrospect it's so foolish masquerading as a seeing man. It takes so much energy!

In that modern building alongside the Iowa River, I was sitting in the cozy seminars with hopeless spectacles on my nose, and fake music in front of me. I was in my self-constructed village of St. Ovide, a blind man in a charade.

• • •

TODAY WE HAVE a marvelous world of adaptive technologies for the blind: Kurzweil reading machines, talking computers, braille, and terminals connecting to the Internet. And most significantly, in the United States we now have the Americans with Disabilities Act, which was signed into law by President Bush in 1990 and is a civil rights guarantee. Nonetheless, princely autocrats still reign on college faculties. Accordingly, higher education is a race. Semesters are timed contests. The speed of absorption is all that counts. In this race the visually impaired are reduced to depraved animals. Books float past our outstretched fingers.

I sit in a sagging chair in Professor Gambrel's office. In my mind's eye he's a failed study in austerity. His scholarly fierceness has gone to seed. The sleeves of his sport coat are too short. His tie is badly knotted.

I lean forward, feeling for the edge of the desk, and begin without knowing precisely what I want to say.

"I'm afraid that I need more time to complete an essay." My voice sounds adenoidal. "It's a question of research really, I've read all the primary material. But you see, the trouble with my type of vision impairment is that I can't read much at any one time."

I have the "To Whom It May Concern" letter in my pocket in the event that this scholar of words needs to read something.

"The need for additional time is not acceptable in graduate school." His voice is throaty, like water I once heard pouring in and out of the exhaust pipe of an old motorboat.

His face drifts before me like a durable pink rose, something from the cemetery.

"Well it's not really a question of acceptability, you know, like we're in the admissions office or the Pentagon. I can't see."

"Then you really shouldn't be here."

"Of course, you're right. And I suppose Milton, Homer, James Joyce, they couldn't have taken a course in this department either?"

"I don't believe you belong in my course!"

Outside, leaning against a brick wall, I feel like throwing up. It's November, but there are still grackles in the vines that cling to the building. I think of how I once told T.J. that grackles live solely on shit. The thought cheers me up. I picture Gambrel and his seventeenth-century men seated together at a conference and snacking on turds.

I will have to get the dean to enforce the law so I can finish the book, the paper, the gestalt. "Hello, Dean Churchspire, I'm afraid, like Spinoza, that I need more time for my monads."

. . .

I SIT UP all night with Hal and Vernon. Three young people awake in a student apartment on a stifling summer night. Hal is from Louisiana, he literally grew up in a vast industrial junkyard. His father's business would sell anything, from used aircraft engines to Chinese tapestries. Hal speaks seven languages fluently, writes inventive and musical poems, and cooks huge beef tongues and peasant soups on his tiny gas stove. He does everything full out, runs marathons, or drives all night just to see a certain strawberry farm at sunrise.

Vernon is not happy in this midwestern college town. He hasn't been able to write for close to a year and stays in the library reading magazines or goes to films. He feels patently dishonest and hands in old work for discussion in the seminars. Someone tells me he looks a little like the British poet Philip Larkin, owlish, sour, bespectacled, heavy.

We have a bottle of aquavit and some Swedish rye crackers. We also have fish roe, pickled herring, and a dish of pickled onions. There's a carton of cigarettes, a bottle of vodka.

Vernon is telling us about the old film studios in Queens, New York.

"The Marx brothers made their movies there; like Woody Allen, they didn't like Hollywood. They thought it was anti-Semitic. You know that famous line of Groucho's, 'I wouldn't belong to a club that would have me as a member'—that wasn't a joke, he tried to join several social clubs, but they wouldn't let him in because he was a Jew. And the Jewish clubs, Groucho couldn't stand those."

"Shit!" says Hal. "Wyin' the hell would Groucho wanna join

clubs? That's *absurd*! That's like a dadaist wanting to become a librarian!"

"You can't have Dada without some books to cut up," I say.

"Yeah, but dadaists find their books on the street."

We smoke with the lights off, a single citron candle gives a votive flicker to our faces. Without lights I really can't identify the simple objects around me and more than once drop my glass or flick my ashes into someone's drink. As a result, Vernon drinks his vodka tonic with ash. He doesn't seem to notice.

After hours of aquavit and vodka Vernon produces something that he describes as opium. Vernon and I smoke it with tobacco and sit until dawn listening to the last songs of Berlioz. The grimy apartment smells of peanut soup and cigarettes. At sunup we walk to the river, imagining somehow that we'll swim.

When I stumble, the others think it's drink. When I fail to see the red hydrant, they assume I'm opiated. Of course. Of course. And the eyes roll in my face, two poisoned grapes in a sea of flesh.

It's quarter to six of a July morning, and Hal is singing some lines by Bertolt Brecht at the top of his lungs.

At the bridge where we intend to jump into the river, we meet an evangelist. He's been up all night "studying," as he puts it. His leaning bicycle has saddlebags stuffed with small paperback Bibles.

"Where you fellas goin'?"

"We are, we three, gathering at this bridge to kill ourselves!" says Vernon. "Our entire family died in a plane crash. We're two of us brothers, and this is our cousin." He points to Hal.

I pipe up, "Cousin Hal hasn't spoken since the accident."

Hal, who is athletic, hops deftly to the top of the bridge's steel railing and starts to walk like an Egyptian tomb figure.

"You don't look like suicides."

"I know," says Vernon, "we're not dead yet."

"Well, I'm not going to let you boys jump off this bridge. It's a forty-foot drop, and there are concrete ledges under the water. If you hit one of those, you *will* be dead, or at least maimed. And if you do miss the concrete under there, the current right here is fast—you could drown slowly, that's one of the worst ways to die."

"Damned if you're not the real thing!" shouts Hal, who jumps down from the rail and ties his shoe. "You make me want to run and run, lift up my bony shanks. I am perfumed with awe!"

He takes off, running. And Vernon and I are suddenly running after him. I'm running faster than I've ever gone before, delirious in our childish escape.

But Hal is nimble: he outdistances us in half a minute. Because I swim, my aerobic conditioning keeps me going, but Vernon drops behind. Suddenly, I find myself running along the river walk like any morning jogger, and as I run, I feel that premonition of great events that the drunk often feel.

I'm lucky that the sidewalks are good and level. I think I can go a long, long way. There are no stark changes in this terrain. I'm safe, flying, arms out, chest pounding. My eyes are like windfall apples, sweet, brilliant, beyond good use. But I'm a wave, a blessing, every part of me oiled. I seem to have left my friend far behind.

Then I hear them, several shouting men. It's a morning work crew. I'm sure of it.

They have just completed a marble-smooth slab of wet concrete! And now I, the greatest runner of them all, Paavo Nurmi, here I am, bounding into their oasis of solidifying work!

I plunge straight in like a great bird with wings and neck outstretched.

I'm falling into the heart of their labor, horrified, constricted, foolish. To my mind, I ought to be a figure of splendor—at least to one man in ten—and then I slide headfirst right through the drying cement.

There is silence.

One of the fellows lifts me to my feet, spins me around.

He's talking spitfire cartoon gibberish.

"What the . . . how the . . . fuckin' . . . didn't you . . . waddya BLIND?!"

I have concrete in my hair and beard. It hangs from my shirt like pelts strung around a fur trapper.

"Yessir." (I'm trying to catch my breath) "I'm blind." I say this quite matter-of-factly, and the deadpan surprises even me. It's like telling a salesman my shoe size.

"Aw shit! Are you telling me you're fucking BLIND?"

"Yeah. It's nuts, jogging like this, I know. Look, I'm sorry, really sorry. I—"

"He's BLIND!" It's as though he's telling the others that I'm his mother. *He's my MOTHER! It's my fuckin' MOTHER right here in our concrete! What're the odds against that?*

"You mean you're jogging like this, and you're *blind*?"

"It's bad judgment. But mostly there's no one out here. Nothing to run in to."

"You do this a lot?"

"Mostly I swim."

"Yeah. When that concrete dries on your leg, I'd love to toss you in the pool!"

In only one minute they've gone from thinking I'm a red tiger of misfortune to believing I'm an imbecile. And now it's becoming clear that I'm yet another creature, a newborn worm in the first snow, a thing with no known grouping.

"Look," says the man who introduces himself as the foreman. "My uncle's blind. He can only see colors. You should get a guide dog. You're nuts to do this. At least jog with a companion." He pauses for a second. "A *sighted* companion!

"You know what my uncle did after he lost most of his sight? He went to the local mall and drove his car in figure eights around the parking lot. He got there and back without a scratch! His wife didn't even know he'd done it! Then he went and got a dog."

Much to my amazement, this guy drives me to my house in a university truck. I wish now that I could remember his name.

"Really, the guide dog's a salvation."

And there I am, back in my apartment, embarrassed, richer, blinking fiercely, fatigue or tears, fighting both, peeling concrete jeans from my thighs, wondering which Buddha that paving man might be.

He probably thought I wasn't really listening. I have a lifelong facial habit, a built-in poker face when I'm listening or, more precisely, when I'm hearing. And as I sit on the floor of the bathroom, the better to scrape concrete from my arms and legs, I sense that a chord has been struck with that notion of a guide dog. But in emotional terms, I'm not a grown-up yet.

I bundle up my ruined clothes and throw them in a Dumpster. My next social security check is coming tomorrow. I'll buy some new jeans and running shoes.

■　■　■

BARRY MEETS ME in the student union cafeteria. He's in a remarkable mood, upbeat, energized. The University has purchased one of the first Kurzweil reading machines for the blind.

"It's an incredible machine," he says, while putting creamer into his coffee.

"It's like a Xerox machine, there's a glass plate and you put books on it. It scans the pages, and then it takes that print information and runs it through an onboard computer, which converts everything to synthetic speech."

"You're joking?"

It's 1980, and I've never heard of computers being used for anything other than missile tracking at the Pentagon or snooping at the IRS.

"Yes," Barry says with his cup at his lips. "There's a microcomputer inside this machine. It takes the photocopied image, and using speech synthesis software, it matches the print with a machine voice. I've read about it, but I haven't heard it. Do you want to have a look?"

My impulse is to joke about this.

"I bet the voice sounds like Nixon, and at night when no one's around, it talks about all the people who've persecuted it."

"Yup, then it tries to pick up the Xerox machine."

On the way to the library Barry unfolds his cane.

"I'm going to travel by example, walk softly, carry a big stick."

"You're braver than I am, Barry. I'm all fucked up."

"Well, I *know* that!"

"I don't know. I just don't know. What *is* it? I suffer from CSS—that's Can't See Shit—but I don't think I could hold a cane in my hand."

"Here's what I think is the deal with you." He stops. We're

standing in a car tunnel underneath some railroad tracks. It's a Saturday morning, and we're the only ones out walking.

"You're afraid to be *seen* as a disabled person even though you have a *huge* vision impairment. I can understand that. All disabled people can. Hell, FDR had an agreement with the press that they wouldn't photograph him in his wheelchair. He thought disability would screw up his image as a strong leader. And you know what? Those days aren't really over for lots of disabled people. Let me tell you, being overtly disabled is like wearing one of those advertising sandwich boards, only instead of "Eat at Joe's," it says, "Look at me! Be afraid! This might happen to you!""

He pauses. A campus security car is slowly rolling by. One of the officers rolls down his window.

"You fellas need some assistance?"

"No thanks," Barry says, then adds, "actually, if you could tell me what time it is, that would be a big help—we're waiting for the library to open."

"It's eight thirty-five. It should have just opened up."

"Great! Thanks!"

It strikes me for the first time just how absolutely poised Barry is, and it dimly occurs to me that the white cane does have positive power. The idea that campus security might actually volunteer assistance has, at least momentarily, widened inside my skull.

"Do people do that often?"

"Sure, all the time. They see the cane and try to help."

"Doesn't it annoy you?"

"Of course, but it depends. In that instance the guy was wondering if I needed directions. And you know what? I often really do need directions. So I weigh it. Other times there are people who see you about to cross a street, and they grab your arm without asking, try to hustle you across like a Secret Service agent shoving the president. It's weird and fantastically annoying. They've made the assumption that blindness is a mental condition. Those are the same people who talk to your friends in restaurants, you know, waiters who take everyone else's order, then pause, look at the blind guy, and say to the assembled sighted folks, "And what will *he* be having?" That stuff can drive you nuts! Or they assume that because you're blind, you can't hear, and they shout at you.

"But you know what? I wouldn't trade any of that away for the struggle that you're living in. For you, when you *do* tell some fucked-up professor you can't see—well, that becomes a struggle, because they don't understand how someone without a cane or dog can be blind. And of course it's none of their fucking business whether you use the cane or not, I know that. But in terms of your safety, and your general ease of passage through the world, I can tell you, it makes a real difference to use the damned thing."

We sit on the library steps while I smoke a twisted Marlboro, the last in my pack.

"Okay, I give in," I say with a jet of smoke, just wanting to shut him up. "Get me a cane."

"I'm not an Orientation and Mobility instructor, so I can't give you cane technique. But I have an extra folding cane, and I think you should carry it in your hand like a staff so that cars know of your situation. Then we'll send someone to show you actual cane techniques."

"All right, but for now I just want to put it into my briefcase."

Barry accedes to this, having won the larger battle.

In the library we find the Kurzweil machine; it's in an office that is difficult to locate. But at last, with lots of wrong turns, we've arrived. The thing is as big as a washing machine.

"They have tapes here that describe how to operate this baby!" Barry says, opening a drawer. And for the next several hours we play with the key card, locate functions, and finally scan a page of text.

Of course for this demonstration, I've chosen a nearly hopeless book, *The Wasteland*, by T. S. Eliot. And with whirrings and chirps, the Kurzweil machine spits up vowels, then sentence fragments, then gibberish, then sentences.

"Well, that's Eliot!" I laugh. "It's perfect!"

The poem is filled with fragments of foreign languages, ancient Greek, odd line breaks, and so on. The machine attacks it like someone with a gun at his head. The voice is metallic and fuzzy, a robot on bennies. It reads and reads and reads and reads. It's practically air-starved as it heads for the end of the page.

Another decade will pass before this machine can read Eliot, and it will be another decade before I unfold the white cane.

■　■　■

I AM GROWING, though. In Iowa City countless poets, painters, sax players, and composers have found not just good listeners but great ones—and I was no different.

With my friend Ken Weisner, a poet and French horn player from Oakland, California, I write a kind of *renga*—a sequenced lyric conversation that we share back and forth, which we have entitled "Twelve Things I Can Do." This is a spirited, comic, Rube Goldberg–style whirligig of a poem, designed to dispel youthful agony. Ken rediscovers the tenderness of his long-dead father, then sees Walt Whitman in an ordinary Greek restaurant—Walt has spinach pie in his beard. Somewhere else, on another page, Willie Mays walks into the corner bar and puts his legendary baseball bat right on the counter and says, "Man, I sure had a good day with this!" For my part, I write a series of dramatic short narratives in the voice of Nikolai Gogol, who sees ghosts, suffers from hypochondria, and tells extravagant lies to everyone.

It's such a luxury to have entire months, even years, to play with the gorgeous nonsense of growing pains. Ken and I, along with several others, sit in the all-night diner where the hamburgers are fat as car tires and the milk shakes are genuine, and in the midst of the midnight long-distance truckers, we talk about Kyoto, the ancient Japanese holy city. Then we're joined by two poets from Macedonia and one from Nigeria, and we're swapping international cigarettes and advertising lingo.

These years in Iowa City offer up nightly narrative collusions for me with poets from every corner of the world. There are poets from mainland China, Indonesia, Turkey, Ireland, and we drink like mad and argue the merits of Neruda or wonder aloud how Russia would have been had Trotsky lived. We sit in rattan chairs in the Tikki Bar and talk about Nazim Hikmet, Osip Mandelstam, and the Egyptian love poems translated by Ezra Pound. We eat nachos and talk about the Vikings, the *Poetic Edda*, the *Vineland Sagas*, the *Kalevala*, the *Mabinogi*, and we're all full of shit and myth and margaritas. Around us, at high volume, is Mick Jagger's "Sympathy for the Devil." Up the street, the local poet, who dubs himself Alphabet Man, climbs to the top of an eight-story hotel, and from the roof he types on a continuous sheet the world's longest poem, which drops down the side of the building.

The entire city is filled with people who are practicing their instruments. In the library's poetry archive an attendant hands me an 1855 edition of *Leaves of Grass*. I put my nose on the page where Whitman himself embossed the type, and I breathe.

10

WITHIN MONTHS OF my graduation from Iowa, I'm awarded a Fulbright grant to Finland. In retrospect, I suppose I was hoping to impress my father by following in his footsteps; he'd been a Fulbright scholar in Helsinki on two separate occasions, lecturing on U.S.–Soviet relations. My goals are far more nebulous. Through hours of eccentric reading in the University of Iowa's library, I've amassed a basic understanding of modern Finnish literature. My grant proposal asserts that a new internationalism has empowered leading poets in Finland. The proposal is immediately accepted as it sounds erudite, but I have some enormous problems ahead of me. Filling the gaps in my knowledge of Finnish grammar will once again require blackboards and small-print textbooks. And more to the point, how will I get around on my own?

I ask my father if he still has friends in Finland who may be able to meet me at the airport. I imagine myself alone and lost, with a year's worth of luggage, my eyes smacked with the greens and purple of a new place.

Most of my father's old colleagues have died, but he knows a friend of a friend who is a magazine editor for a Helsinki weekly. He makes some calls and phones me in Iowa City to say that this distant figure, Mr. Saarinen, will indeed meet me at the airport. I'm intrigued by the fact that he's an editor, and imagine that we'll have a warm conversation about writing.

I board a Finnair DC-10 with a briefcase stuffed full of incomprehensible poems. I'm a twenty-four-year-old pagan believing in an assortment of gods and goddesses, hagiographies, dreambooks, scraps of overheard conversations. I'm a neurasthenic paradox: disabled, quasi-verbal about it, but still sufficiently ashamed to need to hedge my bets. My masculinity is fragile, my ego crawls around blindness like a snail exploring a piece of broken glass.

When I disembark, Mr. Saarinen comes forward in the luggage claim area. I have been traveling for twelve hours and am exhausted. We have an electric moment of mutual regard, and it's clear that this man hates me. He's nearly silent, stiff as a minister in an Ingmar Bergman movie. With my long hair and beard and the dark John Lennon glasses, I'm sure he thinks I belong to the Charles Manson cult.

"You must be Kuusisto," he says. "I'm here to meet you, but this is a terrible day for me."

"Really? I'm sorry. Has something happened?"

"I'm a very busy man, and today I was supposed to go to the antique automobile show. I love those big cars from America, the old ones with the chrome and the whitewalls. Hudsons, Studebakers, Packards . . ."

Now he introduces his friend Mr. Maki. He's a very old man and a bit unsteady. He, too, looks me over, and when I say hello, he says nothing.

On the ride into downtown Helsinki, Saarinen explains that although he had promised my father he would put me up for my first night in a strange country, his plans have changed. Instead he is taking me to an office that he rents.

"There is a cot there, and a radio, and you can use that for the night. There's only one thing I need to tell you. This office is in a tough neighborhood. There are lots of drunks, and so you shouldn't walk very far. It could be dangerous."

While Maki waits in the car, he leads me to a streetfront metal door that is covered with graffiti. Then he hands me the key.

The office is a cell. I can't imagine, as he shows me this place, why anyone would rent it.

"Good-bye," he says, after warning me not to leave the radio on. "You can mail me the key."

Alone in Saarinen's storefront closet, I sit on the folding cot under a bare lightbulb and am saturated by paranoia. I don't think I can go outside. Eventually I fall asleep after eating half a box of rye crackers, which I find on the floor. A whole day passes.

I have a contact at the Ministry of Education, and by daylight I make my way into the streets and wave at the river of cars until a taxi stops. At the Ministry, I'm given another key, this time to my Fulbright apartment. They also hand me a folder containing the dry information that foreigners invariably need.

Helsinki is one of the world's darkest cities, and winter is coming. It's the perfect place for me. I walk gingerly across icy cobblestones and on street corners I press myself to the signposts hoping to decipher my location. In Finland no one thinks this is strange. There are drunks sprawled everywhere. Whenever I think no one is looking, I take a tiny, newly acquired telescope from my pocket and crane my face up at the signs. I'm on Kaleva Street! Oh, quick! Get that telescope back into your pocket! You look crooked and obscure! Look lively!

One morning two drunks accost me. They've clearly made many nights of it, their coats are reeking. They've caught me aiming my telescope up a street pole.

"Hey, boy! You won't find any pussy up there!" Hacking laughter.

They go waggling crazily down the street.

I sway imperceptibly like the street sign.

I walk everywhere in a threefold nimbus of cigarettes, booze, and poetry. The Fulbright Foundation has paid my way; now here I am blindly trying to find a bus, a street, a house. I can read only in short bursts, nosing back and forth. And there is an ache in me like wind through an open door, a complete, unadulterated fervor for poems. The loneliness is Chinese in its clarity, a new moon over the ruined orchard where I find myself alone and very old and in love.

I plan to translate Finnish poetry into English. But of course I can't see a dictionary. At the University of Helsinki I get lost in the Tsarist buildings, lost in the language, lost in the opacities of retinopathy.

I climb on a strange bus thinking I'll learn the city. The bus enters a warehouse district, a land of smokestacks and freight and boarded windows, and then it stops. I put away my telescope and realize somehow that I'm the only passenger, that the driver is belligerently telling me something, something he thinks is important. I'm disconcerted and annoyed, he has roused me from my visually impaired sightseeing.

He's telling me that the bus does not go on, that I have to get off here, and I climb down into the silvery gulf of industrial Helsinki with no idea where I might be. I start running and arrive at a bridge, where I meet a woman who is cursing. For some reason, while handing her my cigarettes, I tell her in English that I am nearly blind.

"Can you see my face?" she asks.

"No," I say, regretting my sudden honesty.

"Come close," she says, and when I follow her instructions, I see she has a bloody nose and skin like sagging leather.

"My husband," she says, "is a vampire."

"I'm sorry," I tell her. "But I must keep going, I have the opposite difficulty, I can't find my way at night. Good-bye!"

In the harbor I meet a drunken man who is garbed in a great-coat like a hussar. He holds in each hand a set of false teeth, and he's selling them. He thrusts them impulsively at people climbing off a trolley. A joker asks him if he has a match.

I buy a set of teeth for a hundred Finnmarks and carry them in my coat. Later I give them to a foreign student and tell him that he can use the teeth to gain instant access to bars and restaurants: you simply go to the head of the queue waiting for entrance and tell the doorman that you are an American dentist, that there has been a dental emergency within. I tell him it works every time.

And of course I know all about bars. My eyes ache, the library is largely beyond me, so I take to holing up with mugs of beer at torrid dives where everyone is in love with booze. There are drinkers at all hours. In the sloping, midwinter Finnish afternoon, reverie gains and anesthesia is a beautiful thing. I am fruitful with exaggeration, telling hundreds of strangers that I am a writer, a poet, a poet from America, and as the prickles of ecstasy zip along the spine, I create subsets of my life, stories about growing up in Kyoto, growing up in Rangoon, the island of Samos. Outside in the gathering dark the traffic builds, window-panes glitter like black ice. Bundled walkers pause at flower stands, looking to bring some color home.

In the *Kalevala*, Vainamoinen, ur-poet of Finnish mythology, visits the land of the dead, hoping to retrieve a word that is missing from one of his spells. He meets Death's daughter, who is stump-shaped and inarticulate. She hands him a mug of beer that has frogs and snakes in it.

I desperately need words, ones that will point my sharp prow toward the great green water of my blindness. How will I get home? My brain is a bellying sail but without compass. I weave down the slick sidewalks leaning with my shoulders, steering away from the gutters.

One afternoon in the University of Helsinki's lunchroom I meet Karina, an American graduate student who comes from a Finnish-American family. Her skills with the Finnish language are superb, and her interests are literary. She's doing a year of independent research. We strike up a natural affinity, what with our shared affection for Finnish literature and our mutual dismay at what a cold and withdrawn city Helsinki really is. We walk along the harbor esplanade with snow on our coats, and we laugh like mad about the seemingly organized repression of Scandinavian cultures.

"The doormen outside the bars are bred at special spawning grounds deep in the forests," I tell her. "They are breast-fed to the music of Wagner. That's what gives them their Teutonic rigidity, their xenophobia!" (The bars, restaurants, and private clubs in Helsinki are not open to free seating. Customers must stand in long lines waiting for a nod from the doorman that they may enter. In their immense, gray uniforms they are horselike—huge and capricious. They're known for letting people into establishments or throwing them into the street for no apparent reason.)

We're working our way to one of my favorite bars. I know each step, every turn. As a virtual infant, I played in this park.

"Did you ever hear the story about Sibelius and the newspaper reporter?" I ask her as we lean over huge steins of beer.

It's a long, apocryphal tale about Sibelius in old age confiding to a foreign reporter that his compositional gifts had derived from the immense size of his penis. I tell the story with locale, time of day, dialogue. It's funny: it makes a great artist look vain and trivial.

How I labor nonsensically through the minutes, testing the limits of self-tolerance. As in Iowa City, I need people to go places with me, but I can't open myself sufficiently to say it. So I entice people into my plans, drinking sprees, tourisms. But needing assistance and failing to disclose it, I must act more sighted, seem jaunty and independent. I dip my head as though I'm reading the map and talk with brio, but inwardly I'm in a swarm of sightless panic. And of course, those who do accompany me are necessarily to be fooled. I am undeniably traveling in a private medieval dumb show.

I'm not without irony. I know how scared I am. But I still believe that if the words are fast and glib, I can defer the truth. Certainly Karina needn't know how potentially helpless I am. This is a pattern in my life. Since Bettina, I've been with several women, been painfully in love with some of them. Because laughter and song come naturally to me, I'm approachable, amusing, often silly. I get away with fantastic shit. I recite from pages I cannot read, or point out sights I cannot see because I wish to be admired. Since my disabled man's impression is that I'm ugly, it's hard for me to understand how these literate and poised young women can find me attractive. I'm simultaneously thrilled and guilty. So I talk and drink, reciting lines of poems, miming the mannerisms of writers I've met.

Karina likes me, and oh, I like her! But my life lacks the greater integration that comes with wandering the galleries of self, pausing to read the hard words about failure, incompleteness, and self-forgiveness. I have no self-forgiveness. I've learned how not to starve myself, learned how to savor the words. But I cannot accept who I am.

I do the worst possible thing and alternately sleep with Karina and run away.

In the midmorning, while there is still daylight, I read a few lines of poetry, then I totter off into the day. I'm all congery and deception because I don't know how to be a disabled man, and there isn't enough single malt Scotch, or Finlandia, to make ballast.

■ ■ ■

IN HELSINKI'S RAILWAY square I am nearly struck by a trolley. Two pedestrians actually lift me into the air, pulling me backward off my feet as the train races past.

I sit on the pavement with my strewn bundles and taste the meat of my heart. A small cluster of bystanders has gathered around me. A large man helps me to my feet. I thank my saviors profusely, and they understand that I'm some kind of foreigner, hapless in the way of all tourists.

"Where are you from?" asks Jorma, one of the men who has helped to save me.

"New York," I whisper, dazzled by shapes.

"Yes," he says, pausing, "there you have subways, they are under the ground. These trolleys are old, but they will kill you very efficiently!"

We bid adieu, each of us returning to our private, dotted stars.

My very walking is selfish: I'm making strangers responsible for my survival. But I'm addicted to appearing independent.

Every step is a lie. Step, lie. Step, lie. My angels are giddy, just beyond the bounds of life, watching me.

In the Kaivopuisto, the park above Helsinki's harbor, I sit on a snowy bench. I'm under a spell, transfixed at the heart of a private storm. Meanwhile, in the earthly weather, the snow is coming thick and fast. The gulls are crying, ships are coming in. The city is alive with wheels, whistles, the laughter of people skiing through the park.

This is the glittering shower of the infinite falling through a very young man's brain in a very dark town.

He wants to be a writer, a scholar, a polymath. One with a far-roving mind. In the library at the university he sits with a thick magnifying lens under an oval of lamplight, struggling to read for twenty minutes at a time. He is ashamed to be seen reading this way. He reads defensively, lifting his head whenever he thinks someone might be looking. He'd rather be thought of as one who naps over a book than one who cannot read it.

In three more years he will purchase a talking personal computer that will help him move into the blind sensorium of language. But now in the freezing park he doesn't know about personal computers. He doesn't know that the stars of heaven have nothing to do with good or ill. Doesn't know that blindness has nothing to do with good or ill. Doesn't know he could be loved and blind. Doesn't know, in the fool's nimbus where he's traveling, there's an illuminated page ahead of him.

I sit and smoke as the fat snowflakes fall on my shoulders.

The trolley is still whispering past my knees.

Step, lie.

. . .

I GO TO a bar with Tauno, a classic drunken poet. We meet one afternoon in the American Library. He's been translating American poets into Finnish—Robert Bly, W. S. Merwin. We drink into the small hours of the morning, and after hours of reciting aloud, I tell him how fragile my eyes are. He says, hoisting his glass, "You are a shaman!"

I hear Simon and Garfunkel in my head. "I'd rather be a hammer than a nail . . ."

"I'd rather be a shaman than a shit! If I only could, I surely would," I sing. We laugh and laugh.

My eyes are aching as they zigzag wildly.

Alone on the street, I stumble and fall. There are donkey's ears growing from my head.

It's a miracle! I climb aboard the last bus of the night. I make it back to my student apartment, shaking, cross-eyed, toxic, shamanic as hell.

I live in guilty expectation that at any moment my telephone will ring, that some Old Testament voice will say, "You are not substantial enough, you are not working hard enough. We see you. You are failing. You are not a true Fulbright scholar. You are no writer. You are no adult. You are no sighted man. You are an empty leather sack."

I need the white cane.

I need people to read to me.

I'd like an afternoon of good tea and poems read aloud.

There's a lovely woman who likes me. I desperately need to cry and tell her how much I need help with the words. The curbs.

But I carry on brazenly, a dictionary model of the fool, and pursue my dangerous course.

■ ■ ■

ONE EVENING I accompany Tauno to a party in an abandoned warehouse. There are hundreds of stumbling drunks under blue strobe lights. There is wild cursing, a vodka punch is being ladled from garbage cans. People are falling over tables, tripping over others who have chosen to sit on the floor. Everyone seems like a human hand grenade. The men and women here are raging drunk.

"These kinds of parties are against the law," Tauno says. "We have to run if the police come!"

There's a hand on my shoulder. Someone else is poking me. The music is like the Sex Pistols, but it's a Finnish band.

"You must drink this," says Tauno, handing me a plastic cup. "The drunks call it table wine, but it's vodka with berries."

As I reach to take the cup, I'm knocked to the floor by a large drunken man who in turn has been pushed from behind.

There's a slow waltz that the dead do—and some of the living. The steps turn them toward the past. Suddenly I'm falling from my bicycle, falling from the edge of the dock at the lake, falling down the stairs. When I arrive at the floor, a building falls across my chest, an immense man whose shirt is streaked with vomit.

There are oaths, sounds of shattering glass, shrieks, shrill laughter.

Tauno takes quite a while to free me from beneath the fallen drunk. Eventually he and another man roll the vomit-man like a log. When they get me on my feet, I find that my face is covered with blood—but it turns out to be the other guy's blood, and I ask Tauno to help me find the water closet.

Instead we find ourselves in an alley. Snow is falling hard, and the air is momentarily cleaner than any air I've breathed before. We stand in the fresh chill, and as I'm feeling my ribs, Tauno gasps.

Across from us is a garbage Dumpster, big as a city bus. There is an open door in its side, and framed in that space is the risen face of a woman who has no hair.

"I have lost my wig," she says. "Can you help me find it?" Without a word Tauno climbs into the Dumpster. I walk from the alley and, totally disoriented, begin making what I hope is my way home.

11

LIKE A FAIRY-TALE character who's awakened from a trance, I find myself in Chapel Hill, North Carolina. The town is hot as a greenhouse, and on my first day there I'm apprehended by a policeman who tells me that I'm jaywalking. As always, I've crossed the street without seeing the light and made my way by judging the traffic sounds. Hoping to avoid a ticket, I admit to him that I can't see, that I ought to be carrying a cane. The information so startles him that he lets me go.

I scarcely know what I'm doing here.

My father believes that I should pursue a Ph.D. in literature. I don't have the presence of mind to say to the world I can barely see and I can't read fast. By now, I really ought to know better.

Since I love the sections in Thomas Wolfe's *Look Homeward, Angel* that describe the springtime serenity of Chapel Hill, I decide to enroll at the University of North Carolina. The trouble is, I am neither physically nor emotionally prepared for the rigors of advanced literary studies. My heart is there, but it won't prove to be enough.

I rent a small apartment from a retired army colonel who insists on being called the Colonel. He's a big, fat yellow stain of a man with a military pension and some real estate. We stand under the oak trees, and he points when I ask him how to find the bookstore.

I walk there through the throng of new students, and the strangeness of the pale green North Carolina morning reaches under my shirt. My pulse is fast. I don't want to be here, but I'm going to the bookstore.

In the poetry department I find a book by Linda Gregg, an American poet whose work I admire. Her new collection is called *Too Bright to See*. Though I can't read the poems in the hard glare of the store, I'll nose through them at home with my magnifying lens.

Later that afternoon, at the registrar's office, I sign up for Old English, Elizabethan poetry, gothic literature of the American South, contemporary critical theory.

At home in bed with the book of poems, I lie back on my pillow and think of all the money I've borrowed to enroll here. Rain is falling through the oak trees. I'm on a plateau, my blindness is exhausting. I own a packing case of books that I can't read, but I'm continuing to make the most out of my twenty-minute forays through their pages. I read like a geologist, seeing quickly into the Paleocene acrostic.

In bed, leaning back, I open Linda Gregg's book.

A razor-sharp bookmark flips out, slicing my one reading eye.

I leap up, wheeling, clutching my face. I've sliced open my eye, my only workable eye!

I lurch to the bathroom and vomit. There are strobe lights in my skull. A lightning-streaked tree blazes in the back of my stabbed eye.

I bang my shins on the unfamiliar furniture.

This is the kind of pain known to torturers. What am I to do? I don't know a soul in town.

My entire fabricated being is gone. Instantly.

In the kitchen I vomit into the sink. Grab wet towels and press them to my eye.

All night I sit in a rocking chair. My eyes dart about uncontrollably.

I know I should call an ambulance. Instead I rock back and forth, reciting parts of poems silently.

" 'Only brooms know the devil still exists.' " (Charles Simic)

" 'When I went out to kill myself / I caught a pack of hoodlums beating up a man.' " (James Wright)

The chair rocks and squeaks.

When daylight comes, I telephone the Colonel, my landlord. He agrees to drive me to the hospital.

There I lie in a darkened room, alone on a gurney for four hours. These four hours offer a return to childhood: I listen to unfamiliar voices, the click of women's shoes in the halls, the talk of strangers.

When the doctor finally comes in, I begin to babble. "Good eye . . . legally blind . . . birth defect . . . too much oxygen . . ." He, however, is brisk, uncommunicative. He puts a salve in my eye and says that the wound should heal in a few days. He covers it with a bandage, then disappears.

"You're free to go," says the nurse.

I never get the chance to tell him that bandaged in this way, I can't see a thing.

The nurse is turning to leave.

I begin weeping. I feel like these are the tears that Buddha said are in the oceans of this world.

Eventually what with the dispensing of Kleenex, she comes to understand that I am blind.

"I don't know my way around the town. I don't know what to do." I'm on the verge of stuttering.

So thoroughly has my life been spent in the service of passing, I have almost no blind skills. I'm a hermit crab without a shell.

She takes my arm and guides me down the hall. At the nurses' station we make a phone call to the university's Office of Disabled Student Services, and eventually Rob appears. He's a specialist in providing support services to disabled students. He drives me home and arranges to assist me with campus orientation, tape-recorded books, letters to professors explaining my particular needs.

After he leaves, I eat a Mexican dinner, drink a can of beer, and telephone my friend Ken Weisner in Iowa City.

"How in the hell can you blind yourself with a book called *Too Bright to See?*" he asks.

"I thought it was the right book," I say, lighting a cigarette. "I mean, you wouldn't blind yourself with something called *Collected Poems*, would you?"

"No, but you might have tried Marvin Bell's *Stars Which See, Stars Which Do Not See.*"

"Well, I've got another eye, but it doesn't really work." By now I'm crying again.

I stay in bed for five days, listening to local public radio. There are neo-Nazis in Greensboro, there's a riot over there. Reagan announces that a nuclear war is winnable.

I lie in the inscrutable opacities of bandages, radios, and Valium, and take a personal inventory.

Until the accident, I imagined myself as a romantic figure, the poet who is nearly blind, the one who requires only a table, a little light, and some silence. In this vision I was heroic. In addition, I'd learned to travel alone in the world even though I couldn't read street signs or the intricate maps in transit systems. I went skiing, played pick-up basketball with the international students at the University of Helsinki even though I couldn't see the fast-moving ball or the hoop. The intrusive facts of disability were nothing more than a bad hour, a lonely walk. They were not places in which to dwell.

In Auden's poem "Woods" he writes: "Guilty intention still looks for a hotel / That wants no details and surrenders none." I wanted to stay in that hotel, writing poems that would be only provisionally about my life and blindness. I think I would have stayed in that hotel for most of my life. My blindness was turning into a subject, and in a sense, I was its object. By means of an accident, I was denied my mastery of a disability that I'd grown to believe I could always govern.

As a child recovering from eye surgery, I pretended to be a pirate, but this new injury hurts too much for fantasy. Even standing or sitting up can make the pulse throb. What's worse is that the eye keeps tearing open. During the months ahead the pain will put me back in bed day after day until I realize I have to leave. My studies are impossible, and the eye is going to take a long time to properly heal.

Where can I possibly go?

I drift. My sister is completing a graduate degree in dance at Sarah Lawrence College, just north of New York City. I visit her, and together we go to Manhattan. Ironically, New York City is a terrific place for blind people to live, but at this stage I don't know that.

Carol leads me through the tunnels of the subway, and we climb or descend stairs, always arriving in new and potentially interesting neighborhoods. Without any formal Orientation and Mobility training all of this independent travel on my sister's part seems like something I could never do. I think New York City is where I'd really like to be, but I have no confidence.

Every night I fill my eye with a salve and worry that it will tear open again. By now I've returned home to temporarily live with my parents, who own an old farmhouse just north of Geneva, New York. I wind up at the local college, Hobart and William Smith, my undergraduate alma mater. They've hired me as an adjunct professor of creative writing, and I'm momentarily grateful. I like teaching, and the tiny campus frees me from encounters with the unfamiliar.

■ ■ ■

I'VE NEVER UNDERSTOOD those writers who deprecate their students. Roethke made fun of his underclass students at Bennington. Nabokov loathed his sluggish American pupils. The list goes on and on. The classroom, however, is my ray of light. The Bible says there is a fatness in heaven, a rich sweetness where the soul can feast. Sharing stories with my students becomes a kind of mutual tasting. I encourage them to read to me, and they do. Not just their own stories but the things they find at random in the library. Talking in this way, we find we can make something larger, you might call it growing room. Just when you think you've acquired some expertise at understanding the power of words, a student comes along who surprises you.

One morning, sitting beside the lakeshore, Don, a college senior whose legs have recently been paralyzed in an accident, reads to me his own Iron Age myth—a magic story in blank verse, a spirit poem of alchemy, metal, motion, and the power of his wheelchair. He's been through surgery, rehab, and therapy, and now he's flying with his own ancient song.

Don is, in fact, a model for me. He does not know how blind I am, or how much his adapting to disability has offered me in the way of pointers. With his Canine Companion dog, Cosmo, a golden retriever who is both gentle and handsome, he makes his way with what I can only call grace.

Others do as well. One, for example, has bulimia and was raped by her father as a young girl. We devise an independent study that she calls "Freud, Food, and Famine." Her journal is a thing of courage, and as she reads it to me, I want to reach through time and squeeze her father's neck with my bare hands. But time is a nautilus shell for her as well as for me, and there's no reaching back. There are only the effects of hard growth.

"Facts are stupid things," I hear a colleague say, and I incorporate this into my lingua franca of daily blind misfortunes. I smack my head on the shower faucet as I'm reaching for the soap, and moments later, drying myself, I walk into the half-opened bathroom door. "Facts are stupid things!" I say aloud. "Facts are stupid things!"

On the stairs I feel for the edge of the top step with my toes, and I count the number of steps. In fact I carry in memory every set of stairs. "Ten, eleven, twelve," heel and toe. This offers a kind of provisional peace, counting and storing every step, or the upraised, frost-heaved slabs of sidewalk. In a dozen steps I know I will arrive at an enormous tree root that has broken through the concrete. This morning, hurrying with an overstuffed briefcase, I will not forget this gothic tree with its buttresses and occult energies. Adjusting my speed, I anticipate its coming in exactly seven steps.

But while thinking of the tree as a cathedral, I've forgotten a step! The magnet of imagination is dangerous. I'm falling now, and for a moment it seems as though the act of falling will last forever. I'm a diver coursing through a great ribbon of tropical water. And the ground? The ground is, alas, harder today. I've scraped my chin and left arm on a sidewalk slate. My bag has flown open, and pages are everywhere. I smell my blood. Now a dog comes running through the wet leaves. He's thrilled to see me, tail wagging, wet nose right in my bloody face. "Kiss kiss kiss!" says the dog. And the leaves, stirred by the wind, say, "Have some cold broth!"

Later, soaking in the tub, I imagine the dead pharaoh Tut-ankhamen moving out into eternity, still wearing his mortal, embalmed, and altogether blue skin. He's learning how to see in a different way, a protognostic visioning that doesn't require light. I wonder if he has to memorize the stars along the way. Or was that the job of the priests? Deep beneath the pyramids I picture them sending out signals to the wandering mummy: "Star on left, comet on right."

I'm a blind mummy, talking to myself as I feel my purple bruises. Rubbing my elbow, I remember Bob and Ray, the radio comedians. They announced one morning the successful launching of the "Bob and Ray satellite." It was designed to orbit the earth at a height of approximately six inches. I am its human companion, circulating the edges of rugs and chairs, whispering past storm grates and parking meters.

12

THE POET JAMES WRIGHT puts it this way: "The moon drops one or two feathers into the field/The dark wheat listens."

On a late spring night the spruce trees and honey locusts are listening, just as I, with my deepening cataracts, sit upright in my rocking chair, listening. I imagine that I hear the silver maples opening their leaves.

After seven good years of teaching, I am unemployed owing to campus cutbacks. My adjunct position has been eliminated. I'm in the stone chair at Luxor, crepuscular, shaking, and very afraid. Who will hire me?

The day answers with its flatness. Nothing happens. The telephone doesn't ring. Outside trucks shift gears, buses stop at the corner.

Like Robinson Crusoe returning to his wrecked ship for a bag of nails and some calico, I return to old habits, looking for a talisman against the future. The inability to read, the dread of traffic, the fear that blind and unemployed I will wind up home-less—these assorted delations and horrors keep me on my couch. I drink Guinness stout, Harp lager, smoke Marlboros, aware that every puff increases my blindness—that free radical damage to the lenses of my eyes speeds up with smoke and drink.

I think abstractions: the tapestries of Paradise, woven without me; the vague, sepulchral room I am going toward, a rooming house of separation. I listen to old opera records, Caruso, Gigli, Schipa—*"Deserto in terra solo"*—the barbarian blood of loneli-ness whooshing through the capillaries behind my ears.

I try to calculate time zones. All my old friends live at great distances from this red brick apartment building in downtown Ithaca, New York, where I've had an apartment for the past few years. Ken is in Santa Cruz, California. He holds two part-time teaching jobs just to pay his mortgage. He's probably driving from one campus to another at just this hour, while I'm pushing a shaggy green flower around the rim of my cup with my out-stretched tongue. This is what I'll do with the rest of my life. I'll lean back in varying rooms and press a cold chrysanthemum to my lips.

My college friend T.J. is a marine biologist. He's on a ship right now, focusing with scientific rectitude on the mysteries of krill. He can't be telephoned. You can't call Darwin to tell him about your living room of whirling snow and Chinese flowers.

Bettina is a peace protester by profession. I think she's in Ireland, a place well suited for her wise and contemptuous spirit. She never did like technology. She doesn't carry mobile phones to sit-ins.

I go through a whole inventory of people. Each is impossible to reach because each has a purpose, eyes, money, a place in the material universe.

Who would hire a blind poet? I picture the advertisement: "Wanted, blind poet for banquets. Must be able to recite from memory stories that exemplify the culture's values while bringing tears to the eyes of the assembled revelers. Must demonstrate a knowledge of stringed instruments and wine tasting."

Is crossing the line from an invisible disability to a visible one the magic moment in the fairy tale? Will the poisoned apple vanish from my throat?

I must find a job. Such questions are beside the point.

■ ■ ■

AT THE UNEMPLOYMENT agency a woman reads my application and grabs my arm as though I might vanish.

"How fast can you type?" she asks. I wonder if there is a market for fast, blind typists.

Faced with the forms I cannot read and squinting terribly in the incandescent light, I feel the hot wire behind my eyes that comes from muscle spasms and tension. Eyes closed, I see the hydrogen atmosphere bursting with sunspots while the case worker tells me about Social Security Disability payments.

So here we are, a legally blind, unemployed "creative writing teacher" who cannot fill out the fine-print forms, and an over-burdened worker who hands me someone else's ID card as I get up to leave.

My dining room table is piled high with bills.

I now inhabit a makeshift world. Calling others is out of the question. I can't afford the phone bill.

"Liebestod." Caruso. Over and over.

I remember the LP cover for the Rex Harrison/Julie Andrews

Broadway production of My *Fair Lady*. As Professor Higgins, Harrison is the marionette-God looking down from his cloud, lifting the arms and legs of Eliza Doolittle with strings. He seems to be keeping her from falling. I must be remembering this picture because of its association with the term *safety net*. I've phoned the vocational rehabilitation office at the New York State Commission for the Blind. Someone there tells me that jobs for the visually impaired are hard to find.

Today a social worker will be coming to my house to teach me how to vacuum my floor.

When she arrives and sees the clutter of depression, she thinks I'm potentially helpless. She takes me by the hand and guides me with the vacuum cleaner through the squares of floor space.

"You are dancing," she says. "Cleaning the floor is like a waltz. Forward, then back. Then left and forward. This way you'll never miss a thing!"

The social worker is in the nearer Nowhere. I am in the farther one. While she talks and pushes my hand on the vacuum, I am carving a magnificent jade elephant inside my head.

She thinks I'm helpless because my floors are dirty.

She thinks it's miraculous that I can shop for myself.

I reach for things in the supermarket in complete obedience to luck. This I do not tell her. "I do fine," I say.

Suddenly I'm afraid she'll take me to the supermarket and show me how to shop.

It's true, I shop like a hungry manatee. For years I've headed down the aisles in an untethered state. Things wind up in my cart.

Dear caseworker, there are so many places for us to go. I've been faking accomplishment all my days. I've been dueling incessantly, shadow against shadow.

Now the caseworker raises my right arm with a string. She's put a blob of glue on my stove. She presses my finger against it. "This is your broil setting."

I can't bring myself to tell her how I cook by intuition.

. . .

I FIND THAT I am juggling so many fears at once that I cannot sleep for eight consecutive nights. Motionless in the cold of my own fatigue, I've developed a new nervous habit: I pull all the hair from my chest. Then after terrible hours of tearing at my skin, I crawl from bed and gather up hair by the handful and carry it to the dustbin.

Soon I'm pulling at my beard and mustache. One night I shave my face clean because I've ruined my beard. I'm standing before the bathroom mirror sobbing and fumbling with the razor.

Under the stage lights of depression, I'm naked, chasing strands of fallen hair. This is how I cross the dunes of night. It's a good thing I've learned how to vacuum! I will work geometrically with the Hoover and pick up every single strand of my beard.

I imagine that I'm opening the vacuum bag and reattaching all this hair to my pink skin. I'll use actor's glue. I will be the philosopher of insomnia. I will presently speak on the neuroaesthetics of the hair follicle as an instrument of the sublime.

Pouring a glass of milk, I press the cold cup to my naked chest, reminding myself that I've been through dark nights before. Touching the cup to my forehead, I remember a trip to Lapland with my friend Ken.

It was November, and the daylight was brief. Outside the windows of the bus one could see the *reino*—the russet-colored moss that serves as the primary food for reindeer. Soon daylight and the *reino* entered a competition for tonal dominance, as if earth and atmosphere were jealous gods fighting before the eyes of mortals. Had the earth atomized into the air, or had the air entered the earth? Was our bus arriving at the earth's core? Such darkness seemed immovable. The world should have stopped.

We were befriended by a drunk, a yellow man with paper skin: his gray hair stood up like a fright wig. He offered us vodka from a screw-top bottle as the bus heaved and bumped through unimaginable blackness.

"What do you like about Finland?" he asked in a tone that implied incredulity. Why would anyone willingly enter such a dismal world?

"We like the stories," I said. "*Kalevals,* songs of magic."

The paper man took a swig of vodka and eyed me. I had the distinct impression that he was a skinny dog and not a man at all.

"The stories are all bullshit," he said. "There is nothing magic around here. People just get sick. Tell me something else."

"Well, Ken here is from California," I said. "People there are in the sunlight all the time. It's too much for them. It's too bright—the oranges just walk up and offer themselves to his hands. It's terrible. His children won't even get out of bed, they've grown enormous, like big cheeses. You can't live that way. So he's here for some restorative darkness."

"You are now joking with me. There is too much dark here."

I felt that he was right, that I was talking like an adolescent. I was spouting nonsense because I could afford to talk. The dog-man seemed to know that in dark places each word has a weighted value, that the very words are coins.

"We're here because we don't know where to go," I said. "We wanted to see the deep north."

"Now you are telling the truth," he said. "Congratulations!"

At four A.M. I pour my milk down the sink and climb back into bed. I haven't the vaguest idea about my true destination.

. . .

THE NEXT MORNING I buy an electric razor so I won't blindly slice my face. On my way home I am stopped by a stranger's hand. There's a squeal of brakes. I've just barely escaped walking into an oncoming car.

At home I sit on the sofa clutching the incomprehensible instructions for the razor in my trembling hands. I think of the Lapland dog-man. "Now you are telling the truth! Congratulations!" I can't get from one point to another. Can't sleep. Can't pray. Can't find intelligence because I am without humility. I can barely bathe.

Why should it take so long for me to like the blind self? I resist it, admit it, then resist again, as though blindness were a fetish, a perverse weakness, a thing I could overcome with the force of will power.

Now I drink a soup made from chrysanthemum blossoms and observe the air in the room cascading like flour or snow. I'm the first priest in the temple at Luxor: he's waiting for a shaft of sunlight to fall across his face because this will tell him everything about the afterlife: the time of its arrival, the scope and breadth of the palaces there, the type of clothing he will need for the journey. The temples of the ancients were cosmological machines, forecasting devices; how the stars crossed the roof or the sunlight fell through the door could tell them everything.

For years I've stumbled through the curricula of academe, always a month behind in the assigned reading. As an adjunct professor, I've managed with the help of students and strong

medicines. The pain of keeping pace has been beyond descrip-
tion. The chrysanthemums calm me, but 800-milligram
ibuprofen tablets keep the molten, starburst eyeballs in their
sockets.

And so I shave and take an aspirin. Then I call the telephone
operator and ask for the number for the New York State Com-
mission for the Blind. I need help walking.

I've needed help all my life.

It's that simple.

13

THE NEXT NIGHT I'm visited by Mike Dillon, a senior Orientation and Mobility specialist for the State of New York. Mike is one of those figures one supposes no longer exists. He's a humanist, curious, widely read, and totally lacking in pretension. His humor puts me in mind of S. J. Perelman. When he sees all my books, he starts talking excitedly about Toni Morrison. This I had not come to expect from the State Commission for the Blind. We go out walking in the autumn darkness. I admit to him my absolute terror of curbs, hurtling bicycles, children's toys, trash can lids, holes and more holes. Speaking with him, I discover how liberating it is to reveal my dread of the ordinary.

He shows me a long, folding white cane with a rubber handle like a golf club. There's a plastic tip on the far end for sensing the changes in the terrain. The whole thing glows in the dark and is surprisingly light. When you don't need it, you can fold it up and put it away.

"Hey, when you use the cane, people get out of your way," he says. "It's magic! Cars slow down. You're making a good move here!"

He hands it to me, and I take it. Finally.

Nothing terrible happens.

He shows me how to use it, sweeping it from side to side like an electronic metal detector.

The paradox is that my cane produces only casual regard. Cars slow for me. An old man on a porch calls out cheerfully.

I'm wrapped in the silence of discovery.

I'm an acrobat walking on the wings of a biplane. I'm both light-headed and somber, bending to a delicate task.

Nothing terrible happens. I can be disabled. On this ordinary street.

I need to touch my hair. I want to feel my own face.

Nothing is ever going to be precisely the same. My cane is a divining rod.

I'm walking in safety at last.

The cane makes a pleasant *tacka-tacka*.

I kind of like it.

Mike promises to visit me again in a week.

The next day, coming home from the gym, clutching my heavy bag and tapping my way up the stairs, I encounter a boy who must be about ten years old. I guess from the sound that he's sliding down the banister to the landing above.

"Are you blind?" he calls down to me.

"Yes," I say, "in a manner of speaking that's true."

"You must be bad!" the kid says then, almost under his breath.

I stand for a second, then keep climbing.

Later a friend points out how people grab their children or step with exaggerated haste to avoid my path. I feel at once lovely and flawed, like the Strangford Apollo.

Strangers want to guide me across the street—one woman approaches in the midst of a snowstorm. She asks if she can help, rather than impulsively grabbing my arm. It turns out we're heading in the same direction across several blocks of ice and badly shoveled sidewalks. Since we're walking side by side, I keep the conversation going: "I feel like a man in a Russian film—you know, one of those high-speed, black and white documentary scenes where the people walk unbelievably fast." She laughs agreeably. "Yeah, I've seen that," she says, "people in huge fur coats."

It's the coldest day in New York State in a century. It's also the last day for me to pay my overdue cable television bill. It's now twenty degrees below zero. I'm being held together by *Star Trek: The Next Generation*, a TV show in which people wearing designer pajamas regularly defy the laws of physics. I don't think I can live through the early evening without the voice of Counselor Troy, an empathic woman who knows what's happening in the hearts of intergalactic strangers. I choose not to tell any of this to my sidewalk companion, who has lost her Chevrolet. She's from Tennessee. I tell her how to find the car. As we're about to part, she says, "My husband just broke his ankle. He's such a crybaby. I told him it's only a broken ankle. I have to find the car now and drive him to the hospital."

On the next street I step aside for two elderly women. One says to the other, "Poor man! And he's so young!"

The other says, "I saw a blind boy just the other day. He was all by himself at the Kmart."

Returning home, I decide to take a bubble bath and listen to

National Public Radio. I hear a woman talking about her experiences with menopause: she has to put her head in the freezer, she feels her body betraying her. What really grabs my attention is her sense of the unfairness of it all; her body is doing this to her too soon, she's old already and still in her early forties.

"Me too!" I shout, waving a soapy loofah. "Me too!" I'm already a very old man!

The woman on the radio says that there should be a cable TV channel for menopausal women and perhaps another one for men in midlife crisis—both groups tend not to sleep much.

Later that night, awake in my bed, I think about a cable channel for the blind. I remember how a fully blind friend of mine once went to a Kmart in Iowa City and made his way to the TV department. He told the salesman that he wanted to buy a large-screen color set. The salesman insisted that all he needed was a seventy-five-dollar black and white set, that the sound would be the same. Dave pointed at the biggest color set: "I'll take that one." "But why?" the salesman asked, almost pleading. "Because blind people have families that like color."

Late at night, awake as usual, I toy with the idea of a television channel for the blind. At first, I have silly revenge fantasies. That is, the programming would inflict on the sighted what the blind invariably experience. But thinking about television, I remember that the public broadcasting channel is now pioneering a video description service for blind viewers. Skilled narrators interpose incisive descriptions of the visual images on the screen between breaks in the soundtrack.

Thinking about the tender voices on PBS and the medium of television, I picture the curve of the earth, and the rising stars, and the stylized rays of broadest energy moving into space. I imagine that somewhere out there exists a planet of the blind, where the video description from earth might be overheard. They, in turn, would send back their own descriptive signals. How marvelous to conceive that our first contact with intelligent life would, in fact, be blind life.

I invoke the planet at three A.M.:

On the planet of the blind, no one needs to be cured. Blindness is another form of music, like the solo clarinet in the mind of Bartók.

On the planet of the blind, the citizens live in the susurrus of cricket wings twinkling in inner space.

You can hear the stars on the windless nights of June.

On the planet of the blind, people talk about what they do not see, like Wallace Stevens, who freely chased tigers in red weather. Here, mistaken identities are not the stuff of farce. Instead, unvexed, the mistaken discover new and friendly adjacent arms to touch.

On this particular planet, the greyhounds get to snooze at last in the tall grass.

The sighted are beloved visitors, their fears of blindness assuaged with fragrant reeds. On the planet of the blind, everyone is free to touch faces, paintings, gardens—even the priests who have come here to retire.

There is no hunger in the belly or in the eyes.

And the furniture is always soft. Chairs and tables are never in the way.

On the planet of the blind, the winds of will are fresh as a Norwegian summer. And the sky is always between moonshine and morning star.

God is edible.

On the planet of the blind self-contempt is a museum.

14

THE EARLY MORNING sunlight falls between the trees like rays of undersea light. I'm moving without seeing the pavement, relying on what the Finns call *sisu*: a word that combines stamina and fate. The whole world closes around me in an impressionist's thicket. I think of the surrealist poet, André Breton, who understood the eroticism of modern art in which part of the world is known and another part is just out of sight.

The cane feels good in my hand. My adjustment to it has been grudging but altogether necessary. I recognize this. With Mike Dillon's encouragement I do not cheat and take the cane with me every time I leave the house. I've been doing this for about a month. But I have to convince myself that the morning air is innocent, that fear is less florid than reality, that the world's red insects will not come flying at my face.

Mike and I go out for a training walk. It's autumn in Ithaca.

The traffic at a four-way intersection is obeying no known rules of civilized flow. The crossing light doesn't work. There are red rubber emergency cones in the middle of the street.

As we step off the curb, a green Chevrolet comes blazing through the stoplight. It's a bright-edged, lethal cloud. Mike pulls me backward.

We stand in the cold air and collect our wits. We're feeling rich with adrenaline.

I've imagined the cane will have a civilizing influence on traffic, and in some sense it does. Still, the world's drivers are not like musicians in an orchestra, and my baton simply isn't grabbing everyone's attention. There's danger out here. I need something more powerful than the cane. I need eyes. Now that I'm out of the closet, and blind for everyone to see, the cane has done all that it can do.

I'm thinking: dog.

We're both shaken by our close call with the Chevy, so Mike suggests we step into a coffee shop.

When we sit down, I ask him about dogs for the blind. I seem to remember a Walt Disney television program about these dogs.

"Don't they evaluate what you're doing?"

"It's known as intelligent disobedience," Mike tells me. "The dog judges whether your decision to cross a street is safe before the two of you proceed. They watch out for everything that might hurt you. Curbs, stairs, skateboards, holes in the pavement. A first-rate guide dog is a beautiful companion."

I sip my coffee, mulling over his words.

"Hey," he says, "women really go after guys with guide dogs!"

"Yes, but with my luck the dog would get the date."

"It's a start."

"What else do they do?"

"They pull you back if a car runs the light. They take evasive action. They watch out for low overhangs. These dogs are rather amazing."

"How come all blind people don't have dogs?"

"Having a dog takes stamina. The dog is on a regular schedule of feeding and care. Also, you have to train with the dog. The guide dog schools are like a kibbutz. You work for a month under the supervision of the trainers who have trained your dog. It's hard work."

"Does the dog actually lead you?"

"Yes and no. You are the navigator. You are always setting the course. The dog pulls slightly, maintaining a kind of sensory pressure between you. If it has to stop or draw you out of the way of something, there's no slack. The harness handle is rigid and made of steel."

"But I'm in charge?"

"You're in charge."

"Unless I'm about to get creamed by a Chevrolet!"

"Exactly."

A life without fear.

I fiddle with my spoon. I see myself walking a city street accompanied by a princely dog, a large, tawny, sinuous lion of a dog. The image is unexpectedly warm, an unanticipated gift. I can feel stirrings of excitement and want to go shopping right away.

I gave up my bicycle in Iowa City years ago. I refuse to give up walking.

I've been living too long in rural upstate New York, and I feel confined in these little towns. I want desperately to go places and travel in a new way. If the guide dog school is like boot camp, so be it.

I rack up a massive phone bill by calling friends across the country. I phone Bettina in Ireland.

"I'm getting a guide dog! And I can go everywhere with it—even to the Metropolitan Opera!"

We laugh about this, unsure whether opera is a form of animal cruelty.

My friend David Weiss tells me I have a great dog gestalt. And I believe him.

Not everyone reacts with optimism.

My mother initially sees this decision as something sad. We talk it over, both of us darkened by the years.

"There's no heartbreak here," I say, trying to help her sense how freeing this is for me. How hopeful.

"I want to travel everywhere. This dog will be my constant companion. She'll be my eyes."

The word *blind* still bothers my mother. I've learned it's fruitless to expect her to react to my disability any other way.

I go to the health club and run for forty minutes on a treadmill. Then I feel my way among the weight machines with my cane and lift some weights. Afterward, sweaty and happy, I talk with Dan, a club trainer whose good sense of humor I've learned to trust.

"I've decided to trade my cane in for a dog," I tell him. "This damned thing just won't come when I call."

Dan has a friend in Texas who owns a guide dog, and Dan tells me that the dog has changed his life.

I find myself engaged in my own talking cure, as if the power of assertion and my newfound enthusiasm can instantly overcome twenty-five years of objection.

Back home, on my sofa, I think about this as-yet-wholly-imaginary guide dog school. I see it as an old-style institution high on a hill, protected by iron gates. It's a Dickensian place, and in the fictional abstract it frightens me. Regardless of my bravado, I'm insecure. Still, the prospect of attending a school called Guiding Eyes for the Blind is a crossing I must make to reach the mythic dog. Without Mike's support for my decision, I couldn't have proceeded. I would likely have stayed on my sofa with those antiquated opera records, Caruso's voice coursing through me like quinine. But like the arms of a windmill, trust can scarcely be heard. It begins with conviction. Mike pushes me forward with assurance and his own brand of expedient humor.

Some weeks later, I'm visited by Dave See, a representative from Guiding Eyes. His name is perfect. He teases me and puts me at my ease. Dave's job is to conduct a home interview. Basically, he's here to see where I live and find out how I travel. By learning how fast I walk and with what degree of certainty, he can begin the process of matching me with a dog even before I go to the school.

"It says on your application that you have trouble navigating at night. Why in the hell do you want to go out at night?"

By now I have trouble navigating by day.

We go outside and plan a course for our practice walk. Dave observes me as I work with my cane, then asks me to wear a blindfold and go a few blocks, again with the cane.

"It's sometimes the case that blind people who possess some residual vision can rely too much on that vision when training with a dog," he says. "You must give all your faith to the guide dog and let the dog make the decisions once you've given her directions about which way to go.

"At Guiding Eyes a trainer may decide that you are resisting giving that trust to your dog, and they might ask you to wear a blindfold. I need to see how you'll do."

I walk blindfolded up Cayuga Street in downtown Ithaca on a wet February morning. My cane sweeps the path, and my torso dips forward as if I'm wearing a bag of bird shot around my neck. But I move along safely and with reasonable effectiveness. Dave See and Mike Dillon follow behind but at some distance. I feel like Orpheus climbing out of Hades: I want to turn around and ask how it's going, but the rules are firm, and I walk with a plodding diligence, stepping in puddles, never quite knowing when to stop.

After the blindfold walk, Dave hands me a guide dog's harness. "I'm going to be your guide dog," he says. "My name is Juno."

I am to grasp the handle of the harness while Dave holds the front.

"I want you to lift the handle and say, 'Juno, forward!' and as we move, I want you to trust Juno's every step. Follow the harness. Put your trust in your dog guide."

Dave begins to pull, and I follow. He draws me around a pothole, and I follow. We arrive at a curb, and he stops, and I say, "Good dog!" with a sweetened intonation that will prove important when I am paired with a real dog.

Trust is silent as the windmill. Life with a dog will begin my alchemical transformation in blindness, *la vita nuova*. The harness will unite us in confidence and guardianship. Working with Dave does not yet suggest this.

Back at my apartment he gives me a boot camp spiel about sacrifice, hard work, long hours, life with a roommate, the criticism of trainers, the possibility that I might not get a dog at all.

He explains the daily routine. Every morning I'll be awakened by a loudspeaker at six A.M. I must take the dog outside, then bring her in, feed her, and take her back out again. I'll have a half hour to shave and shower before breakfast. Immediately after the eggs and coffee I'll have an obedience class with my dog and a short lecture about dog handling. Then I'll board a bus for a day of field work—different traffic situations in the company of a trainer. My dog will already know what to do, and my job will be to learn how to work beside her. At the end of the day, the dog must be fed and walked again. Then there's dinner and an evening lecture. I'm to be in bed by ten P.M.—a good night's sleep is necessary. The whole process begins again the next day—and for twenty-five days after that.

Dave's descriptive challenge moves me to fortitude. I will be one of the ones to survive the canine kibbutz and emerge with a companion. I am absolutely convinced. Nothing can induce me to turn back now.

II

—

MOTION

. . . If we propose
A large-sculptured, platonic person,
free from time,
And imagine for him the speech he
cannot speak,
A form, then, protected from the
battering, may
Mature: A capable being may re-
place
Dark horse and walker walking rap-
idly.

> —Wallace Stevens,
> "The Pure Good of Theory"

15

AT GUIDING EYES there are soldiers from Israel, a scientist, a schoolteacher, an auto mechanic, a carpenter. . . .

We have diabetes, glaucoma, retinopathy of prematurity, cataracts, war wounds. . . . We are a democratic group.

One of us is rich. Some of us are very poor.

One goes to AA.

One woman who plans to become a social worker refers to the blind as "blindies."

One is afraid of dogs, but she is going to overcome it.

One is a connoisseur of beer.

One of us hears a brutal drumming in his ears wherever he goes.

All of us have been lost, fallen down stairs, driven cars on wild sprees, had flings with gluttony, God, and a hundred other fumbled embraces.

Some of us still know how to play.

One of us bought a motorcycle when he went blind. He goes out in his yard each morning and turns the key and stands listening to the Harley sounds.

Hank, my roommate, is a study in profound survival. He lost his eyes in a shooting accident. Bird shot in his eyes, some in the front of his brain. Then he had a stroke. He taught himself to return to the world of speech by singing in his head, remembering the lyrics of song.

We sit on opposite sides of our dorm room, which smells faintly of floor polish and wool blankets, and we share Fig Newtons and listen for instructions from the intercom. We unpack our suitcases feeling as if we're in a barracks. Outside in the hallway people move past slowly feeling the walls.

Hank is recently blind. His eyes are hand-painted and made of plastic. He wins my affection right away by telling me how he dropped one of his eyes on the floor at the school for the blind he'd been forced to attend back in North Carolina. His description of groping for an eye on the floor is sheer poetry.

He is happy that I can see a little, figuring that I might find his dropped eyes before he steps on them.

We laugh over my story about a girlfriend who dropped her diaphragm—before she could retrieve it, her dog raced up and ate it.

Then I tell him about T.J., who woke in the night and drank a cup of bedside water, only to discover in the morning that he'd swallowed his girlfriend's contact lenses.

We imagine our dogs picking up the dropped stuff in our lives.

A new world.

In the hallways the doors are brightly painted in orange, red, yellow. For those like me who must make their way in permanent smoke, walking here is like a dream and then a waking. I'm here, exactly, at this door. I've found where I need to be.

This is in fact my first experience with a place that has been built for blind people. Room numbers are raised and three dimensional and very large. Braille is on everything, from the candy machines to the exercise machines. Telephone numbers are printed in braille and in large print. Walking around, I begin to understand that guesswork is overrated. The memorized phone number, the entire shopping list, these were my specialties. I begin sensing that I can put some of this behind me.

My damned brain can be freed from its inching memorization.

In the lounge, where the instructors give evening lectures, chairs are arranged along the walls so that the large carpeted central area of the room is "blind friendly." The furniture itself is never rearranged: you can count on the chairs and tables remaining in their principal places. Doors are never left ajar. In the dining room the salt and pepper, Tabasco sauce, milk and water, each has its spot on the table.

But these are only the beginning of many wonders for me. In the rec room after our first supper several of us get to laughing. Blindness can be appreciated for its sub rosa comedies, its hidden worlds of amusement. Only the blind can sense how foolish the sighted world's patterned responses to blindness really are.

Tom is from Chicago, and like the city itself, he has broad shoulders. He's a weight lifter and marathon runner. Like me, he can see just enough to appreciate the odd human-shaped shadows that approach him on the sidewalk.

"What I like to do is lurch toward the people who are doing everything they can to get off the sidewalk so I can pass. You know, those people who see you coming with the white cane and they flatten themselves against the walls of buildings or jump into the gutter. When that happens, I can't help myself, and I go into this crab-walk thing, where I lurch right off the sidewalk while flailing with my cane. I'll follow them right into the storm drain like some kind of human train wreck. I can't see their faces, can't even see what in the hell they look like, but I can tell they're backing up and preparing to run. It's like they're in a monster movie and the human fly is coming right at 'em!"

"Yeah, well, they're afraid that you'll bump them, and then they'll be blind too—everyone knows that blindness is like a game of freeze tag!" This came from Sarah, a high-school teacher from California who is returning to Guiding Eyes for her second guide dog.

"You mean blindness *isn't* like freeze tag?" says Roy, a college student from Boston.

"I like it when you're in an elevator and the door opens on some floor, and the sighted person who's standing there won't get on," says Mary from Philadelphia.

"Is that because of the dog?" I ask, thinking that some people are afraid of all dogs, even guide dogs.

"No, I mean this was when I had a cane," she says.

"Yeah, well, you didn't mention the gun you were holding," says Bill.

"Did you know that blind people can legally buy guns?" says Hank. "There's nothing in the gun application about blindness."

"Don't you think a blind army would be a great idea?"

"No, the Italians tried it."

Now Terry, who is from Texas, tells us about driving a car long after he was declared legally blind.

"I told the cop that I'm blind and that's why I'm driving in circles in the parking lot, and you know, it's an abandoned shopping mall and there are no cars, so what the hell? And then he let me go!"

"Waddya mean, he let you go? You mean he just let you drive away?"

"No, he drove me home! I think he thought I was the wildest guy he'd ever seen."

"He probably thought you'd be a bad influence on the rest of the jail."

"What I like about the sighted world," says Bill, "is that they think blindness affects your hearing, so they shout at you—'*Do you need to use the bathroom, honey?*'—a waitress shouted this at me while I was standing beside the bathroom waiting for my wife. I wanted to shout back, '*No, no, thank you, I don't use the bathroom anymore!*'"

"I was giving a presentation about guide dogs at a grade school," says Mary, "and a little girl asked me, 'How do blind people find the toilet?'"

"What did you tell her?" I ask.

"I didn't really have an answer."

"It's a prayer thing," says Hank. "Blind people pray their way to the toilet. That's how I always find it. 'Dear Jesus, let me find the loo, for I am in great need!'"

"I thought that's what the guide dog is for," says Bill. "C'mon, Champ, find the toity!"

"Guide dogs are geniuses," says Gary. Gary came to Guiding Eyes for his first guide dog in 1963. "I was on this beach near Santa Cruz, and I let my guide dog walk loose, even though you're not supposed to, and all of a sudden, here he comes with a bikini top in his mouth!"

"That's a retriever!"

"Do dogs like that take extra time to train?"

"Well, you know," Gary continues, "dogs will pick up anything. I had another dog bring me a live baby crow. She just put it into my hand. The crow didn't know what to do. I didn't know what to do. The dog didn't know what to do."

"My first dog once picked up a carnation. A red flower. Right out of a street vendor's stand. Carried the flower right down the street!"

"I want a dog that finds money," says Hank.

"Hell, I just want a dog," says Gary. "The cane's a miserable way to travel."

■ ■ ■

THE NEXT MORNING we gather in the courtyard to work with the trainers who guide us around the grounds. Each trainer has four students. Each holds a leather harness and plays the part of a guide dog. We practice commands for sitting the dogs, making them stay; we snap the training collar so the trainers can see how strong we are. Out in the kennels are dozens of fully trained guide dogs, waiting to be carefully chosen for each one of us.

Each successful team has a family behind it who actually raised the dog. Imagine loving an animal for over a year and then one morning you get up and put it into a crate and drive it to the airport and send it to the guide dog school. And as you're driving home past the fast food restaurants and shopping malls, you're crying. This dog has been everywhere with you: gone to work with you, gone to the high school football game.

Now what should you hope for?

You're sitting at a stoplight, the tears streaming down your cheeks.

You know there's a chance that the dog won't make it. Maybe

this dog will come home again! Should you dare to hope for such a thing? Is it all right to think this—at least in private?

Imagine that your minivan still has a blanket on the floor. The car still has some prized dog hair and a faint, wet dog smell.

It's okay to hope the dog comes home. Isn't it?

Alas for you, there is a form of goodness that Dante described as "ardor." It's a spiritual practice, a gift to the world that is in turn a part of eternity.

Ardor.

If you're a blind man or woman, you may meet the people who raised your dog. You may form a bond, become a kind of extended family. Maybe not. Perhaps you might be shy, or your sense of maintaining a personal connection with your guide dog is necessarily a private thing. But no matter how you live, you have learned something about ardor.

■ ■ ■

THERE IS NO analogy to getting a guide dog. Holding the leather and metal harness and walking with Lynne Robertson, I feel as if my hands have been waiting for this—as if I've touched something central in the life of an ancestor. The sureness of the handle is like picking up the first chestnut all over again. I know Lynne is guiding me safely around the grounds. She's talking to me as we go.

"Your dog will also talk with you," she says as though she's reading my mind. "Really, the dog's body language and the information you'll receive from the position of the harness will be very important."

I sense that the Guiding Eyes training process is a ritual. First the novice commands an imaginary dog. Then we hold empty harnesses, like farmers who have sold their oxen. Finally after two days of observation, the trainers repair to a secret location to matchmake the students with their future dogs.

I tell Lynne that I need a dog who will be a cheerful frequent flyer—one who can handle either Manhattan or New Hampshire's woods.

I've taken the slow way to blindness, resisting it like a suspicious skater who fears the river. But no one here wastes any time explaining how they can't see, or how they can see a little. All the trainers are knowledgeable about the many types of blindness. Even the housekeeping staff has been through in-service training and has tried on occluding spectacles that replicate the varieties of vision loss. Everyone who works here has walked the building and grounds repeatedly under the conditions of blindness.

Imagine an institution that is really built on trust!

I drink Pepsi and talk long into the night with Hank. We both want to go places. We both have a planet hunger.

Because Hank had a sighted adolescence, he tells me about driving, wild nights on the back roads of North Carolina. Every now and then he lets out a confidential laugh, and I know he's remembering something hot. He's a native storyteller.

I tell him about life without driving, about trying to fit in and not succeeding.

We talk about Carolina.

We talk about motorcycles.

We hardly get any sleep.

. . .

IT'S DOG DAY!

Hank is up at six A.M. as excited as a child on Christmas morning—he's talking on the phone, checking out the weather, doing a wild inventory of life—absorbing whatever happens to be at hand. It's been snowing hard, now it's sleeting. A plane has skidded off the runway at LaGuardia—twenty-four people were injured. Hank guesses we won't be going to town today. Dogs are on the horizon. It's dog day. Hank is like Eisenhower before the Normandy invasion—every nuance of weather is central.

Dog day. Showers and water pipes and doors slamming all over the building long before the regulation wake-up call.

The trainers assemble us, and one by one we're told the name and gender of our dog. I'm told that my dog is Corky, a female yellow Labrador retriever. Then we're sent back to our rooms, each of us filled with suspense, each wondering about the new life to come, a life where the circle of blindness will be entered by a smart and reliable animal. How large will my dog be? Will she like me? How long will the bonding take? Can I trust my life to this heretofore imaginary creature?

The training staff knows each dog as an individual. Every dog has characteristics that will make a good match with a student.

Some dogs are fast, others slow. Some are temperamentally suited for working in the city, while others might do well in urban situations as occasional tourists but really shine in small-town settings. Guiding Eyes has dogs that are especially suited for working with human partners who have multiple disabilities. These dogs are taught to compensate for balance problems, for example, by adjusting their gait. Some dogs are trained to help people who are blind and deaf—they have good command of hand signals. The entire kennel is full of guide dogs who individually possess special skills.

Waiting for the dog call is unlike any experience I've ever known. I find myself alone in my room revisiting periods of my life. I'm on the esplanade in Helsinki bumping into strangers, though I'm not drunk. I'm climbing up a flight of stairs in the New York subway system. Am I with my sister? Or alone? I'm entering a harbor in Greece, and Bettina is exulting about the temple on the hillside, and the sunset, and I see none of it. I want to leave images like these behind. These last moments, pre-dog, defy description. I know that in the next few hours my life will be forever changed.

Suddenly the loudspeaker crackles, and my name is called. Lynne Robertson brings me into a special lounge with curtained doors at the far end. I sit in a straight-backed chair, and Rick Connell, the supervising trainer, hands me a brand-new leash.

"When Corky comes in, she's going to be very excited, and she'll probably jump all over you. Just take a little time to be your silly self with her. After you've had a few minutes, you can put the leash on and heel her back to your room." Lynne Robertson, the trainer who will work with me, tells me to call, "Corky."

There's a breeze from the far end of the room. The sliding doors open, and I can hear the curtains billowing. When I call Corky's name, my voice catches. I have to call her twice. I hear a sound like the snorting of a horse, and the musical dog tags, and then she's on top of me, her paws on my knees, her immense head straight in my face. I'm unprepared for the speed of it. This dog is kissing me. Her tail is banging like a rope. Tears are literally running down my face. She's a twenty-five-thousand-dollar dog, intelligent and superbly trained. But she's been kept in a kennel in advance of our meeting, her own loneliness has been honed.

I have the sensation that Corky is genuinely observing me, but the gaze is more encompassing than that of a pet dog. She seems to be absorbing me.

Janet Surman, a trainer, says suddenly, "Corky's in love."

I snap on Corky's leash, and we walk together for the first time back to our room.

It's the definitive blind date!

Corky is absolutely wild with excitement, and at eighty pounds, she's powerful. I think suddenly that I've been given a fake dog, or that Corky is in fact so astute that she's reflecting my own nervousness. Now she's standing over me nibbling my nose. Then she puts her front paws on my shoulders and starts on the rest of my face. Her tail knocks things off a chair.

Words are loose inside me, the lines from Stevens: "The angel flew round in the garden / The garden flew round with the clouds . . ."

Corky and I are romping like William Blake's emancipated chimney sweeps, freed from their soot and sporting in the air.

Soon I lie down beside her on the floor and begin talking.

"I tell you what, Cork: Let's you and me take care of each other. Let's go places! How do you like that idea?"

Tail wag.

"We'll use our common head!"

Tail wag.

"Your ears are so soft, they have no analogy.

"Hey, Cork: I bet you like to swim. We're going to New Hampshire in two months."

The tail.

By now my voice is a running wave.

This really is a date. We're learning about each other. We go outside, and I find that unlike the other guide dogs, Corky needs cajoling, even some singing from me, before she'll pee. The other guide dogs fidget and attempt to socialize with each other, but Corky is perfectly still. She's ready for this job.

On our first night together she demonstrates another part of her personality. Unlike Hank's dog, who sleeps contentedly through the night, Corky tries repeatedly to climb in bed with me. This is not permissible, according to the training rules, and I hiss at her in the dark. "Get down!"

She ignores me and wags her tail.

At four A.M. I begin to worry that the dog may be too goofy for this job.

The next morning in White Plains, Corky pulls me back from a Jeep that is cutting the curb.

She moves straight back. With strength.

Two pedestrians applaud. One says she'd like to get a guide dog too. I laugh. But I can taste my lungs, as if I've been running in Pamplona.

For the first time I feel the sunken lanes under my feet.

The street is more my own. I belong here.

I'm walking without the fight-or-flee gunslinger crouch that has been the lifelong measure of blindness.

I'm not frightened by the general onslaught of sensation.

The harness is a transmitter, the dog is confident.

At every curb we come to a reliable and firm stop. I cannot fall.

At Guiding Eyes the operative phrase is, "A little stubbornness is a good thing in a guide dog!" When I think of this, I'll always be standing with Kathy Zubrycki, a senior trainer, on a cold March morning in White Plains, New York. We are with Corky at the sheer edge of a railway platform. There's a ten-foot drop to the tracks below.

Kathy is telling me how Corky will not let me walk off the platform, and I listen in a bone-chilling wind with my collar turned up and my left hand on the harness. Behind us a train roars past on its way to New York City.

"Go on," says Kathy, "tell her to go forward."

"I think I'll just wait for the train to get here. I feel like going to Poughkeepsie!"

"Go on now. Corky isn't going to let anything happen to you, and neither am I."

I tell her that I believe the dog will prevent me from walking off the platform, that I believe Corky is as good as her noble reputation, that she, Kathy Zubrycki, has a wonderful voice, a beautiful voice. I am babbling like Woody Allen.

Inwardly I'm thinking, "What if the dog belongs to a suicide cult?"

Then I laugh and exhort Corky to go forward.

She yanks me backward, turns, walks me in the opposite direction until we are safely away from the tracks.

Faith moves from belief into conviction, then to certainty.

We are a self-conferred powerhouse, we two.

At age thirty-nine I learn to walk upright.

With the help of classmates and the trainers, I am choosing to be blind in a forceful way. I even begin to enjoy my mistakes.

One night when my sister is visiting the school, I walk into a screen door. Janet Surman sees this and says, "You looked really good coming through that screen!"

I know it's true!

Nothing like this has ever happened to me.

I am among sighted people who respect blindness.

There isn't an ounce of the patronizing or the sentimental in this. They work you hard when you're in residence, and they admire your breakthroughs: I am evaluated as a guide dog team.

We work on and off the subways near Lincoln Center.

On a midtown bus the driver actually asks me where I want to get off.

We walk through a complicated and noisy construction site. Corky is absolutely in focus, in harness, in tandem, in control.

She's not afraid of the jackhammer.

She rides on escalators like Marlene Dietrich, all poise, greeting her public.

Back at Guiding Eyes she distinguishes herself by passing the famous "jelly doughnut test." The trainers have placed doughnuts and slices of pepperoni pizza around the training center. As we walk through the hallways, she pays them no attention and even guides me around them!

I suspect this dog reads the encyclopedia in her spare time.

At Pace University she circles around a tethered goat, leads me past a flock of loud geese. She stops at the top of a flight of stairs, even though a donkey is braying just behind an adjacent fence.

She takes me carefully through a Japanese garden.

We walk through an arbor where a hundred birds are singing.

We belong in this territory, she seems to say, and my own joints loosen. We slip through the unfamiliar with balance. Entanglements of harsh light do not slow us.

We work together through a revolving door into a mall.

All the while we're followed by Lynne or Janet, who applaud our successes and warn us of problems.

"Don't let her pull you that hard," Janet says. "Use the 'steady' command."

She shows me how to move the harness forward and back as a signal to slow the pace.

Corky slows. She's suddenly distracted by a parakeet in a pet store window!

"Tell her to 'hop up'!"

And now Corky refocuses, turns back to work.

Why didn't I yield to this earlier? Why did I take so long?

It doesn't matter. I'm doing it now.

We're moving fast!

Dave See was right. This partnership requires discipline and precision. The payoff is self-reliance and faith.

In a cavernous, shadowy department store I'm moving swiftly through abutments of stacked perfumes.

We pass what must be a line of women's coats. To me, they seem like a herd of white deer, a chorus line of dancing egrets. I don't know what the hell they are, but while I'm wondering about it, Corky is taking me around a huge wreath on a tripod that is precisely in the middle of the aisle.

I may be moving in fog, but nothing is going to puncture my life vest. I'm sailing through Macy's!

We shamble near the television sets, and I can hear a football game in progress. The salesman comes forward and admires the dog. Then he shares his game narrative with me. As he talks about the Dolphins, I discover that I'm not on my private adolescent raft. My new boat holds playfully to the river. The other boats signal me with their steam whistles.

Theodore Roethke wrote: "My eyes extend beyond the farthest bloom of the waves; / I lose and find myself in the long water; / I am gathered together once more; / I embrace the world."

■ ■ ■

ON SUNDAY, MARCH 27, 1994, I board a USAir flight from LaGuardia Airport in New York City to Ithaca, with Corky at my side. Lynne Robertson, who has accompanied us on every day of training and watched us grow into a safe, working twosome, comes with us to the boarding gate.

"Okay, Corkster," Lynne says, "you look after this guy."

And then I'm walking down the gangway with Ms. Corky in the lead, and we enter the cabin of the plane. And our new life, which will be spent entirely together, has begun.

For the foreseeable future, Corky and I will be supported by artists fellowships. Within months of our graduation from Guiding Eyes, we take up residency at the MacDowell Colony for the Arts in Peterborough, New Hampshire. Corky lies next to me on the braided rug of our forest cabin, and soon we're making noises together, visceral tunes, bone music, rubbing our backs, each of us growling. It's good, the dog and man making sounds together, and the exhausted parts fall away.

16

_____

WHEN ONE HAS been returned to life, everything is compelling, but for me the mornings are the best thing of all. At dawn, Corky gets me up out of my disheveled bed by tugging the blankets. While I'm getting to my feet, she returns with one of my running shoes. We've come to New York City to visit my sister, who now lives in Greenwich Village, within a short walking distance of Washington Square Park. Corky is prancing around the living room of Carol's apartment, still holding the shoe in her mouth, as if it were a living bird. She's ready for life beyond the door.

On Fifth Avenue the world tickles us. What a thrill to hear a horse's hooves at sunrise! Here comes a mounted policeman! Corky stands stock still, erect, making sure I don't step into the street. The freshness of the hour circles and sways around me. I didn't know the dog would bring me the morning.

I smell bread from a French bakery, chestnuts roasting, the wet skins of oranges. At the center of this sensorium is the soft jangle of Corky's harness, a striving music like a tiny breeze along a mast.

Now on Fifth Avenue with aching, foggy eyes, I can walk without trying to see. I close my eyelids and move as smoothly as a dragon in a child's story.

■ ■ ■

MY FIRST TWO years with Corky create dotted lines all over the United States. In Santa Cruz, California, we walk along the boardwalk and have our photo taken while sitting inside a Hollywood mockup of a mammoth killer shark. The Polaroid shows the dog sitting outside the shark's mouth. She'd refused to climb inside the silly gaping jaws. The dog's face seems to say, "This man is beneath all regard." Underneath the picture I scrawl, "Intelligent Disobedience in Action"—then I send the photo to Guiding Eyes.

In San Francisco's Chinatown a very old man stops me and says, "That dog has such love for you. I can see it!" Then he walks away, his blessing conferred.

On Bourbon Street in New Orleans we're hailed by a Dixieland jazz band: "For our special guest we'd like to perform 'Yellow Dog Blues'!" Applause breaks out around the bar. When the band takes a break, I tell them that Corky is a big fan of W. C. Handy's work.

This guide dog brings me a curious liberation. Like a buoyant swimmer, I'm secure as we move where the ocean is hundreds of fathoms deep. Often strangers will swim along beside us and say a few words before they vanish. Guide dogs are still wondrous creatures in the public's imagination, and more than fifty years after their introduction to the United States, they remain a novelty.

While standing in line in the post office in Peterborough, for example, I overhear two local men who have obviously taken delight at seeing us.

"I've never actually seen a guide dog!" says the first.

"Me neither," says the other, "but I hear they can do everything!"

I imagine he thinks the dog will retrieve a can of beer or a midnight snack.

"I hear they know thousands of words."

"I wonder how the dog knows where he needs to go?"

I'd like to tell them that although we move as one, we are more than that. Guide dogs and their human partners must each trust the other's bravery and judgment. The dog travels where I've decided we should go. The blind who move in this way must have exceptional orientational skills. Having chosen our direction, I confidently let Corky make all the navigation choices. Only fifty percent of the dogs who are bred and raised at Guiding Eyes successfully complete the training. Each certified guide dog is preeminent in the canine world.

On the street we are a magnet for those who once knew a blind person, or who have a blind family member, or know someone who is going blind. On Lexington Avenue in Manhattan a businessman asks me how to get help for his wife who has been diagnosed with retinitis pigmentosa. We're at the curb waiting for the light when he notices how I check the time with my braille watch by opening its hinged crystal and feeling the raised dots on the face.

"That's such a beautiful thing!" he says. "I've never seen anything like it. I don't mean to intrude, but my wife is going blind, and I've been trying to learn about ways of adjusting."

"I'll tell you what," I say. "Let the dog concentrate on this street crossing, and then I can talk."

On the far side we discuss the correct mechanics for crossing the street.

"I need to focus at crossings," I tell him. "I'm the one who makes the decision about when to cross, not the dog. So I must listen carefully to the traffic flow. When I think it's safe I command the dog to move forward. At that point the dog evaluates the command by checking it against what the cars are doing. The whole procedure demands our combined attention."

"You know, all these years, when I've seen a blind person with a guide dog, I thought the dog was watching the streetlights! I believed it was the dog who ran the whole show! I never stopped to think of it as a partnership!"

And so here we are, two strangers and a dog standing on the corner of Lexington and Fifty-second Street discussing how to keep going.

I walk away from him thinking about the challenge that he and his wife are going through. No two blind people are alike. I, for instance, grew up wearing chains like Houdini, trying to pull off a magic trick. Not everyone with vision loss goes through this long struggle with self-consciousness. There are those who lose their vision suddenly and find tremendous powers of resilience. They give hope to the people around them, both the sighted and the blind.

We are, all of us, ecstatic creatures, capable of joyous mercy to the self and to others. The strong blind move like modern dancers, their every gesture means something. The newly blind or the lifelong blind often possess an art of living, an invisible, delicate vessel that they carry. The sighted can have it too: José Carreras comes to mind. After his bout with leukemia, he still sings, and though some critics say that the great tenor's voice is not the same, I say it is more thrilling, touched as it is with buds of darkness. Sometimes roses grow on the sheer banks of the sea cliff.

■ ■ ■

HOW STRANGE IT is, sometimes, to be Corky's human appendage. Often people stop our forward progress and speak only to her, as if I do not exist, then, after much baby talk, they vanish. Others are drawn to us because we are totemic. Early one morning I meet two boys with developmental disabilities.

"Hi!" one says. "I knew a blind guy, but he died!"

"He was bigger than you," the other adds. "He had a heart attack!" Then they sweep away down the sidewalk on their Rollerblades, and through it all Corky advances without distraction, my familiar, my Pavlova.

In the supermarket we're spotted by a small child.

"Look, Mommy, there's a dog in the store!"

"Shhhh! Be quiet, dear!"

"But Mommy, that man has a *dog*!"

"That's a blind man! The dog helps him."

"Is the dog blind too?"

"No, the dog sees for the man!"

"What happens if the dog is blind?"

"The dog isn't blind, honey, the dog can see. It's the man who can't see!"

"The man can't see?"

"That's right, blind people can't see."

"If he can't see, how does he know when it's morning?"

"Shhhh! Be quiet! The man gets up because he has to have breakfast!"

The woman hurries her little boy down the cleaning products aisle. I hear his thin voice from some distance.

"How does he eat?"

I'm standing beside an enormous pyramid of cans. Corky has decided to sit down. I have an evangelical desire, a need to reassure these two. I want to recite something from Psalms to them: "The Lord is gracious, and full of compassion; slow to anger, and of great mercy."

I want to follow this mother and child through the tall laundry soap displays and tell them that the world doesn't end. I imagine telling them that the blind are not hungry for objects. I want to take strangers by the hand and tell them there is no abyss.

Under the tower of Coke cans Corky and I pause, and I wonder about the discrepancy between my blindness as a symbol for others and the reality that I'm not all blind people. I'm only one man, a slightly bent and middle-aged man with a bad back. I've been successfully guided here by an exceptionally beautiful dog. I suspect that we may look accomplished, but behind this tableau—man and dog—I'm as lost as any of you. In fact, I'm more lost. I've entered this supermarket because I need something for lunch, and though I'm here now, I require help to find the tuna fish.

This business of shopping can be hard. Unemployed, I pay for my purchases with food stamps. Such transactions are hard enough for the sighted—food stamps are an embarrassment. At the register, the impatient cashier has to take my booklets and count them out for me. The line of customers is stalled behind us. A child steps on Corky's tail. There's an overall impression, unspoken, shared by everyone in the line, that of course blind people have no money.

For over a year Corky and I have been living back in Ithaca and looking for a job, attending employment workshops and seminars, sitting in the Labor Department under the buzzing fluorescent lights. Seventy percent of the blind remain unemployed in the United States. This fact is a source of pessimism, both for me and the social workers who try to help as I fill out forms for state sponsored medical assistance, state sponsored job counseling, state sponsored hope. As I tend to my paper work I can hear from an adjoining room an angry mother shouting at her crying child.

Outside, walking through the fallen red maple leaves in a public park I think of fortune tellers and imagine Theocritus standing beside the sea. The old, Greek diviner pours water through a sieve and surmises the shape of the future by watching rivulets of water on the sand. Is there a stream from the sieve that's longer than my dull, personal sorrow? Theocritus, will I discover the joyous striving that necessarily defines a strong and good life?

Corky flops on her back and rolls in a huge pile of fallen leaves. Leaves are in my hair.

What is the future?

Legend has it that the prophets of old went to their respective caves and slept, dreaming of sunbeams. A forceful, prophetic dreamer might stay asleep for over fifty years.

Will it take fifty years for me to find a job?

Fate it seems is made of thorns and blossoms and bones. As Corky flings leaves and growls with satisfaction I contemplate gloom. The future is indifferent to emotion: events unfold with or without our melancholy or optimism. But there must be sufficient reason for optimism, and for the sentiment that we can craft our potential lives.

The park; twilight; a cold breeze . . .

Beside a granite war memorial two teenagers are smoking marijuana. I hear them talking together, their voices like recitative in opera: expressive, musical laughter in the dark. Somewhere, in one of the letters of Horace, the Roman orator and poet, he says that the ears provide less nourishment to the human soul than the eyes. I suppose the assertion was true in the pagan world, the world before Bach.

Corky stands and I put her harness on. We walk in the nighttime freshness. At the center of the city, there is a waterfall that tumbles through a steep gorge. Corky guides me along a narrow path. The world here has a rich, mossy scent and the roar of the falls is thrilling. I stop in the autumn night beneath the immensity of sunless stones—a place that has always been without direct light.

. . .

IN THE MORNING over coffee I talk to my dog. In turn, the dog is wise enough to ignore me.

"Let us go to Manhattan, Corky, and loose our barbaric yawps from the rooftops!"

The dog does not raise her head in expectation. She is not a Disney creature.

"Let's walk across the Brooklyn Bridge."

Corky goes to the door when I pick up the leash and harness.

New York City is an extraordinary place for walking, particularly when you have time. Job seekers have time. I find myself returning to Manhattan over and over again. The topsy-turvy play of light and movement is a climacteric therapy for a depressed blind man who is hagridden by the Fates. Walking in New York I realize I can't spend my days in the failing offices of rural labor departments.

The Brooklyn Bridge has a civilized, old-fashioned promenade deck, with teak benches and intricate wrought iron lamp posts. This walkway is sensational, crossing the bridge at its highest altitude. Cars and trains are far below, half heard through the wind. Out here, trembling like a compass needle, I tilt my face in the glorious light. I'm wearing the darkest glasses because my eyes ache where there is brilliance, but the light is perfection, the naked sun coming closer now as if Corky and I are prayerful gnostics who have silently identified the proper secret names for air and sunlight.

My eyes fill with violet silhouettes, tricks of the air, shapes made by the cables of the bridge, a cluster of grapes hanging in the open air. No, it's a turn of the century gas light, still standing out here. I'm stock-still, filling myself—every microscopic and meandering raindrop inside a man must be replenished with another. I picture myself holding the sieve of Theocritus above my head, the water falling in streams through my hair.

It occurs to me that my experience of the Brooklyn Bridge is so completely cerebral it is in fact a kind of metaphor, an imaginary headdress like those body-length hats worn by Tibetan women. In my version, the bridge falls over me in layers of amethyst, gold, purple and silver. These are the threads of being.

● ● ●

CORKY AND I walk all day. Our private Manhattan is cross-stitched with red and black passions. The zeal to live moves us here and there like paper boats. I enter a Russian jewelry shop and buy a tiny, ornate, Orthodox crucifix from a very old woman. I struggle to give her my money—she wants me to take the cross as a gift. When she does take my money it's a tearful moment; I've spoiled her act of charity, an act that comes all the way from the Ukraine, a gesture that has crossed a century and an ocean. Outside on Seventh Avenue I'm suddenly weak in the knees and wander without direction for a time.

On lower Broadway two young black men see me walking with Corky. One pokes the other.

"Man," he says, "why they let motherfuckers like that out on the street?"

I have no answer.

Half a block later I want to tell him that I fought for his civil rights—why the fuck doesn't he fight for mine? By now I'm beginning to weep. I wanted to be splendid this afternoon. I have a brand-new opera from Tower Records in my bag, Saint-Saëns's *Samson et Dalila*.

There's an archive photograph of Caruso as the blinded Samson in the act of raising his dreadful, newly blinded face.

I too want to pull down the temple.

I step off Broadway into a Greek coffee shop. I sit at a table, and Corky lies down. I overhear two waiters discussing which one is going to wait on me.

"You do it," one says to the other, "you read him the menu."

"You know," I tell the waiter, "you really have a clean, well-lighted place here."

Sometimes I imagine that my younger selves are with me around a table. I tell them that acknowledging blindness has meant something that was formerly unimaginable. There's power that comes with admitting how little I can see because the world is more open and admits me far more graciously than it did when I was in the closet. But it's hard in a different way. You are watched everywhere you go, and sometimes I feel buried beneath the graffiti of other people's superstitions.

In a taxi I hear the driver mumbling, and instinctively I lean forward to catch his words. Do I mind if he asks me a question? His tone is a somber whisper, like that of a man who will soon make a deathbed confession. By his accent, I guess he's from Haiti.

He tells me how his aunt lost her sight—he snaps his fingers. That's how fast it was.

"Does she have friends?

"Does she have people to help her?

"How are her spirits?"

These are my questions, but it turns out that we're not talking about his aunt at all—we're navigating the realm of sudden blindness—the land of dark spells.

"She was a beautiful girl," he says, "nice hair, nice teeth, very fine! Let me tell you she was a beauty. But she goes with the voodoo man, even though the voodoo man has a wife, she goes with him. She cooks for him and looks after him. Everyone tells her not to have anything to do with this man, but she don't listen—she spends all her time with the voodoo man. One day when the voodoo man's wife is gone, she goes to his house and tells him that she's going to clean up. She opens the door to the voodoo man's closet. She could feel a wind blow right through her head, and then she was *blind*!"

As the cab races down Fifth Avenue, I ask him again if his aunt has people to look after her. "No," he says, "no one will go near her—she has the voodoo now."

In a shop in Greenwich Village a woman hands me a stone. "This will help you," she says. "It's a bloodstone."

"What makes you think I need help? Do I look like I need help?"

"Being blind can't be easy," she says. "This stone is known to have soothing properties."

"I didn't really come in here to be soothed," I say. "My sister is over there buying some earrings."

"I think you should have this stone!"

She presses it into my hand.

I want to tell her the dark has its own sunlight. But I'm trapped. She believes I need a cure. If I argue, I'll look unwell. I wait behind the frosted windows of my cataracts and finger the tiny stone.

Should I say thank you?

Should I tell her that grass grows from the eyes of the dead Viking kings? The eyes are circled by mascara. Or that birch trees grow from the eyes of Antero Vipunen, the dead shaman who sleeps under the Finnish woods?

■ ■ ■

AS I WRITE, the news has been full of stories about Sheik Abdel Rahman, who is always described as "the blind Egyptian fundamentalist cleric." Several of his followers were suspects in the March 1993 bombing of the World Trade Center.

The Sheik is a flawless personification of blind rage. To the West, this is the fury of Saladin against the Crusades. Abdel Rahman's contagiousness excites the media. He touches others and renders them blind with wrath.

Sometimes the Sheik is seen without his glasses. His eyes are frightening with their smoky blue cataracts. He is disfigured. He has true metaphoric power. This is the absolute blindness of the Cyclops who hurls boulders into the sea.

The Sheik also represents criminal blindness, an atavistic memory from the collective unconscious. The Roman emperors poured lye and vinegar into the eyes of the Christians. The Christians tied ropes around the necks of Muslims until their eyes popped from their sockets. The Norman kings blinded their enemies by holding hot metal plates against the victim's eyes.

Perhaps the most renowned story about blindness is that of Tiresias, who goes blind because the gods are playing a game of sexual trivia. Hera and Zeus argue about the satisfactions of sex: Zeus believes that women derive greater pleasure from intercourse than men. Hera believes otherwise. They decide to call on Tiresias, a mortal who, owing to a magic spell, has been both a man and a woman. Tiresias confirms that women experience more enjoyment—an answer that infuriates Hera, who hates to lose arguments with Zeus. She blinds Tiresias as a punishment. Zeus takes pity on the man, and though he is helpless to alleviate the blindness, he gives Tiresias the power of prophecy. The physical blindness of Tiresias is obscured by the magic of his gift. Actual blindness is repressed and dismissed. Who needs material vision when there is a paranormal and superior kind? Blindness is a good thing, after all. Tiresias is identified with ecstasy, grace, astonishment, instinct, hallucination, the soul.

Blindness and the soul and the judgments of God form a palimpsest. No real blind person can avoid the inner prickles of discomfort that accompany this metaphysical terrain.

Sometimes I lie awake and fuss about matters of the spirit. In this state I often resort to my childhood obsession with hair pulling. Outside in the cold April night the trees make astonishing sounds: the wood has warmed by day, and now the temperature has dropped below twenty degrees Fahrenheit. A tremendous wind has begun, driving dry branches against the sides of the house.

My thoughts run together like watercolors. Lying on my right side and clutching my knees, I hear upsurges in the wind. I can't define what faith is, and listening to the storm I suddenly picture my paternal grandfather, a Finnish Lutheran minister who emigrated to the upper peninsula of Michigan and preached to the woodcutters. I imagine him running between the trees and grabbing at flying shreds of the New Testament; tiny scraps of old Bibles are blowing among the roots and the gooseberry bushes. His faith was always unshakable.

I remember reading something in one of Kurt Vonnegut's books about faith. He said that faith is just faith in faith. Vonnegut imagines that this is delusional. I see my grandfather, his vestments caught in the chokecherry twigs as he reaches for his pages.

Recently I was up late with a group of seven blind men and women. Our tears flowed together like the pitch that binds the boards in a wooden boat. Each of them had lost their loyal and life-affirming guide dog to cancer or old age. So what is faith? One stricken woman who was sitting alone in a corner of the room suddenly said that God only gives you the burdens you can carry. There was a murmur of assent from the others. I remembered some lines from one of Theodore Roethke's notebooks: "What's the winter for? To remember love."

I don't know. I'm turning over and over in bed. Rain has now joined the April wind, and it strikes at the picture window with wild force. I wish I could console people. I find myself thinking about Jesus. Why did he cure the blind in his lifetime, rewarding their faith before the unbelieving multitudes? Now he's silent on the matter. But I've found that I can't live without faith; still its inexplicable rules keep me awake, and I'm more than a little angry.

Early one morning while shaving, I see a televangelist on TV in New York City. Here on my screen is this little man screaming about faith. Before him on the stage is a man who is purported to be blind.

"This man has *faith*!"

Instantly I snap off my electric razor, nauseated with outrage. The studio audience is applauding.

"This is *faith*, my friends!" The evangelist's voice is as slick as a roasting bird. "*Faith* can move mountains!"

The actor who is playing the blind man has stepped back from the preacher and is gazing upward in rapture. I wonder which drama school he graduated from.

Saint Augustine wrote about the necessity of reason in the journey toward God. We all wish to be transported to the divine in one easy step, but reason is endowed with great discernment: it can tell the false sounds from the true. To be alive is to be in adversity. Prudence, temperance, fortitude, and justice can only exist side by side with misfortune. But then I think this is too stoic, for I've discovered love from unforeseen sources. I try to hold on to the words from John, chapter one: "Beloved, now are we, the sons of God, and it does not yet appear what we shall be."

Epilogue

IN JUNE 1995 Corky and I find ourselves back at Guiding Eyes, this time as employees. I've been placed in charge of Student Services. My job is to converse with blind people around the world and to oversee the admissions program and health services. Corky's job is to be Corky. She walks among the guide dogs in training as if to say: "This is what you can become."

In reality, we've learned that we don't have to be symbols for anyone. It's enough to believe in dignified travel and a future that holds out possibilities. Corky and I have become frequent flyers. We are poised to go forward and belong to what's ahead. As we go, we repel the steel filings of anger and superstition.

Still, life with a cane or guide dog is not a fairy tale. I am blind for others, and this carries a thousand signifiers.

There was the priest who tried to sneak past me during the Eucharist.

There was the madwoman at a bank machine who began cursing, "You damned disabled people with your dogs!" She shoved me.

There was the security guard at a midtown Manhattan computer store who tried to prevent me from entering.

There are the street people who try to harass my dog while she's working in traffic.

There was the barber in a downtown Chicago hotel who refused to cut my hair. He didn't want the dog in his shop. "You wouldn't know what a haircut looks like anyway," he said.

There are the strange waiters who rush up, thrust the food in front of you, and run away.

Let them disperse. I have to let them go.

• • •

ONE NIGHT, RUSHING to catch a train at Grand Central Station, Corky and I are accosted by a stranger. He's much like the proverbial cartoon figure who holds a sign warning of the world's end.

"Did you know that the end is coming?" he asks in an oddly childlike voice.

I clutch Corky's leash and suddenly find that I'm laughing.

"No, it's not!"

I begin dancing with the dog.

"No, it's not! No, it's not!"

I am chanting and dancing with a jumping dog.

Some tourists snap our picture, blind man and dancing dog under the big clock in Grand Central. Rush hour going on all around us.

The millennial soothsayer walks away without another word.

Acknowledgments

I wish to acknowledge the generous assistance of the PEN American Center, the Blue Mountain Center, the MacDowell Colony, Villa Montalo, and the Virginia Center for the Creative Arts.

Selections from this book have appeared (sometimes in different forms) in *Antioch Review*; *The Bookpress*; *Harper's*; *The Prose Poem*; *Seneca Review*; and *Quarry West*.

All the superstitions about blindness to which I refer in this book can be found in *The Oxford Dictionary of Superstitions*.

Many of the facts about the lives of the blind in the ancient world come from a long-out-of-print volume entitled *From Homer to Helen Keller*, by Richard Slayton French, Ph.D., published in 1932 by the American Foundation for the Blind.

I wish to thank Leslie Rosen of the American Foundation for the Blind for her generous research assistance.

Many friends have helped me during the writing of this book. I owe special thanks to Rick Abbott, Bill Badger, Connie Connell, Signe Hammer, Patricia Hutton, Carol Kuusisto, David Reilly, Deborah Tall, Ken Weisner, and David Weiss.

Crucial help was provided to me by my agent, Irene Skolnick, and my editor, Susan Kamil.

This manuscript was prepared using the Sounding Board speech synthesizer and Vocal-Eyes speech software from G. W. Micro, Inc. Both were installed in a Toshiba laptop computer, which worked faithfully through power surges.

I owe thanks to Karl Wokan and Mike Dillon from the New York State Commission for the Blind.

I also wish to thank Dr. Catherine Latham and Dr. Cynthia Miller.

Many graduates of Guiding Eyes for the Blind have been helpful during the preparation of this manuscript. I wish to thank Peter Altschul, Rose Marie McCaffery, and Mary Beth Metzger for their advice.

My greatest debt of gratitude is to the Burkett family of Fairfax, Virginia. Bill, Reba, Bill Jr. and his sister Anne Marie raised my guide dog. And then they let her go.